Teacher Education in India
Issues and Perspectives

R. C. Srivastava

2020
Regency Publications
A Division of
Astral International Pvt. Ltd.
New Delhi – 110 002

First Published, 1997

Reprinted, 2020

ISBN 9788186030394

Published by : **Regency Publications**
A Division of
Astral International Pvt. Ltd.
– ISO 9001:2015 Certified Company –
4736/23, Ansari Road, Darya Ganj
New Delhi-110 002
Ph. 011-43549197, 23278134
E-mail: info@astralint.com
Website: www.astralint.com

Digitally Printed at : **Replika Press Pvt. Ltd.**

Preface

The first two decades after independence had witnessed considerable quantitative expansion of education but this had been largely independent of qualitative development in the field. After increase in the number of schools and the enrolments therein, steps had to be taken for qualitative improvement in education. As a result of the recommendations of the Mudaliar Commission on Secondary Education an attempt was made to improve and strengthen the in-service education of teachers with the establishment of the All-India Council for Secondary Education and later on the Directorate of Extension Programmes in Secondary Education (DEPSE) which set up a large network of Extension Services Centres attached to several training colleges and Departments of Education in the Universities to affect improvement in the quality and standard of school education. However, even with the formation of the Department of Field Services in the National Council of Educational Research and Training, the task of extension education has not been very productive.

In the backdrop of these experiences, and following the publication of Baljit-Singh's book entitled 'Education As Investment', and the Education Commission (1966). Report, coupled with the ever expanding demands made on teachers in the context of the changed need of the society, serious attention was given to pre-service teacher preparation beginning with the sixties. Many innovations in the structure, organisation, methods, programmes and practices, in other words, the curriculum including the controlling authorities for teacher education have been worked out.

This research oriented book based on an in-depth study of secondary teacher training institutions affiliated to ten universities in north India, surveys the various facets of teacher preparation and systematically documents the generalizations made from the study of these institutions selected according to five classified systems of practice teaching evaluation (two institutions from each of the five types) followed in the institution. Data for the study were collected with the help of intensive interviews and discussions with the principals/heads of the college/department of Education, teachers and students for eliciting actual information and opinions on all the principal aspects (philosophy, programmes and practices) of teacher preparation. Content analysis of the prospectus, syllabus and other related records and proformas used in the institution also yielded the required information. The book has thus attempted to highlight the current trend in teacher education by analysing the problems and issues in teacher education and the reactions of educational administrators, teacher educators and student-teachers to the way these problems are dealt with in teacher-training institutions.

Teacher education is offered as a course of study in almost all the teachers' colleges and departments of Education of the universities in India somewhere as a compulsory full/part of a paper and somewhere as a full elective subject of study at the M.Ed./B.Ed. levels. The book has not been written keeping in mind the syllabus of any particular university, for any examination, and therefore, in the strict sense of the term, it may not be a text book. The contents of the book however is such that it will be found useful by teacher-educators, student-teachers, educational administrators, and all those concerned with the preparation of teachers. The book covers all the important aspects of the theory and practice of teacher education. It contains discussions on issues, like the philosophy of teacher education, types of teacher-training programme, admission procedure, curriculum, place of student-teaching in teacher education, objectives and organization of student teaching, guidance and supervision of student teaching, evaluating student-teachers' performance, and in addition an overview of development of teacher education in India, coupled with in-service teacher education and some recent attempts to improve teacher education programme and practice.

Whatever may be the merit of this publication if it stimulates thinking on the problems and issues pertaining to teacher-preparation in India, my labour will be amply rewarded. I will welcome observations and comments from readers.

Several persons have contributed to this publication and it is not possible to name all of them. My most sincere acknowledgement is due to Prof. K. Bose formerly Dean, Faculty of Education, University of Delhi without whose contribution in the preparation of the manuscript the book would not have taken the present form. In fact her contribution merits co-authorship. My acknowledgement is also due to the various respondent groups from the teacher-training institutions who shared their thoughts and ideas with the writer on various issues discussed in the book. It will not be out of place to thank Mr. A.K. Verma, the Managing Director of the Regency Publications, New Delhi for undertaking the publication of the book and bringing the same out in print with promptness and in such a fine form.

New Delhi
December, 1996

R.C. Srivastava

Contents

1

An Overview of Development of Teacher Education in India

Teaching — A Skill

'Teachers to be taught and trained' — is a relatively growing concept found in societies all over the world, in the nineteenth and twentieth century. Also it is acknowledged that prior to this period, in all countries and communities teaching existed as a necessary art. Much before any need for special group of people as teachers was felt, they in their varied form, and for varied pattern of jobs made their presence felt. While the parents and elders taught the youngsters in the art of living and doing, inside the home and in the community, the tribal head, the craftsman and the skilled worker controlled the imparting of the special skill to individuals with as much sincerity, austerity and devotion as was necessary. The teacher and the learner entered into the joint venture with utmost eagerness and willingness. The technique of the teacher which was based often on his acquired experiences in the practice of that skill, gradually got transmitted into the learner who used to be declared qualified not by any institution or organisation but by the teacher alone. The testimony of the worth of such transmission lay entirely on the merit of the pupil's or learner's use of the skill learnt. The teacher's recognition came automatically from the learner's performances.

Religious Teaching

The second phase ushered in the period of religious teaching. This time a greater caution was observed in assigning the task of teaching and in assuming the role of a teacher. Priesthood in a rather intangible domain utilised largely knowledge, experience and skill in impressing upon the listeners. Evidently the teaching-learning process touched less of the secular fields and concentrated more on spiritual sphere specifically on the teaching of sacred literature and religious rituals. The measure of effectiveness of such communication between the priest and the disciples or followers was hardly pronounced; it was felt and realised with the observation of the practice of religious rituals.

Indian Teacher

(a) Ancient past

In India, looking back at the ancient past the teacher's role combined both the aspect of worldly welfare and spiritual gain of the learner. Hence the teacher, the guru, was held in high esteem and 'teaching' as a task was widely revered. While on the one hand the teacher was expected to be the master of specific branch or branches of studies, he was on the other hand expected to have a high moral character. Traces as found in the Rig Veda pronounce that for the preparation of such teachers it was necessary that the teacher had to have a scholarly bent of mind, high degree of intelligence and devotion to acquire perfect mastery of the subject; he had to live through an austere life to assimilate the essence as embodied in the subject matter of study (curriculum); he had to live the life of a brahmacharin; and he was an ardent aspirant of the supreme good. Such qualities and education used to go to the 'preparation' of a real teacher who ought to be a good man himself.

Such a person could not deal with 'inert' ideas, could not deal with things impractical. He had to realise within himself the truth of every bit of knowledge by going through it himself. Only then he was in a position to lead the learner to similar paths of realisation. The test of his ability was seen in his skill of teaching. He had to explain and expand, expose and expound, illustrate and interpret, themes and knowledge with the help of his own experiences. This realistic approach to the teaching which combined theoretical base and practical explanation proved extremely worthwhile. Disciples flocked around the efficient preceptor. Though there was no formal rejection the less wanted ones were evidently the less effective teachers. It is clear thus that 'practice' in teaching yielded much more meaning to the truth of 'theory' of learning. However, in the later classical period much adherence to rules about studies and mechanical practice along certain prescriptions brought in for the first time unfortunate emphasis on traditional learning. Still, no formal teacher training course existed, nor any formal recognition to a practitioner through awarding of certificates was in vogue anywhere.

(b) Medieval period

The much-talked of 'monitorial' system that was found in vogue in India of fourteenth and fifteenth century had its early traces in the 'Jatakas'. The expert eye of the preceptor used to detect the few talented scholars who were senior in intellect, and bent on pursuit of knowledge. This small group, it seems, got some impetus from their teachers who would detain them in the school for a longer period and make them competent to take over charge of the younger and the mediocre pupils. This batch of monitors, the intermediaries, so to say, gained gradually in maturity and knowledge, acquired ability in taking charge of the younger colleague and this brought in an element of teacher training for the first time in the history of teacher education. The true teacher was conceived to be one who was well-versed in scriptures and theology, skilful in the art of exposition and one who had acquired a well-integrated personality and commanded respects all around.

This practice of monitorial system as found during the 'Jataka' period could not be free from certain deteriorating influences. Howsoever, skilfully the monitors got chosen by the preceptor, and howsosoever skilful was the care and education of the preceptors in preparing the monitors as teachers, it was seen, the purpose of disseminating learning was not as efficiently achieved as it was expected. Besides the scripture commentaries having risen to volumes and varieties, the learning depended on memorisation rather than logical reasoning, exposition and interpretation. Doubtless to say, the spirit of learning, warmth and welfare suffered a setback. Learning and 'practice-in-assisting-in-learning' became mechanical, stereotyped pursuit bereft of any enjoyment and spiritual gain.

(c) Early british period

The continuation and spread of teacher education in the country down the centuries should be seen primarily in the background of the education pattern prevalent from time to time. The system of indigenous education that continued in this soil throughout the long period of history finds copious mention in papers and correspondences exchanged between the Members of the Board of Directors and those of the Public Instructions of the East India Company ever since they took over the charge of administration in general and education in particular. With all the weakness that had crept into the then prevalent system, some obvious merits were discerned and appreciated by them. The teacher preparation question assumed a special significance in the light of some of their observations. In one instance, G.L. Prendergast[1] (1827) observed, "I need hardly mention what every Member of the Board knows as well as I do, that there is hardly a village, great or small, throughout our territories in which there is not at least one school, and in larger villages more; many in every town, and in large cities in every division where young natives are taught reading, writing and arithmetic, upon a system so economical, from a handful or two of grain to perhaps a rupee per month to the schoolmaster, according to the ability of the parents, and at the same time so simple and effectual, that there is hardly a cultivator or petty dealer who is not competent to keep his own accounts with a degree of accuracy in my opinion, beyond what we meet with amongst the lower orders in our own country; whilst the more splendid dealers and bankers keep their books with a degree of ease, conciseness and clearness I rather think fully equal to those of any British merchant."

1. A.N. Basu. Indian Education in Parliamentary Papers, Part I, p. 125, Asia Publishing House, Calcutta, 1952.

Quoting the above utterance A.N. Basu[2] writes, "Apparently William Adam was not the only one who believed in the existence of a widespread system of indigenous education in the pre-British period. The extract also shows that, defective as the indigenous system might have been in some respects, it was not without its merits."

This view got further supported by many British officers. Of the many, A.D. Campbell's[3] (then the Collector of Bellary, Madras) Report incorporates quite a detailed account of the spread and qualitative standard of education in that district. There were 533 schools (primary) containing no more than 6,641 scholars, or about 12 to each school[4].... "Besides these there are 23 places of instruction attended by Brahmins exclusively in which some of the Hindoo sciences, such as theology, astronomy, logic and law are still imperfectly taught in the Sanskrit language."[5]

"In these places of Sanskrit instruction in the Hindoo sciences, attended by youths and often by persons far advanced in life, education is conducted on a plan entirely different from that pursued in the schools, in which children are taught reading, writing, and arithmetic only, in the several vernacular dialects of the country."

"Some children continue at school only five years, the parents through poverty or other circumstances, being often obliged to take them away, and consequently in such cases the merest smattering of an education is obtained; where parents can afford it, and take a lively interest in the culture of their children's minds, they not infrequently continue at school as long as 14 and 15 years."

"When the whole (scholars) are assembled, the scholars according to their number and attainments, are divided into several classes, the lower ones of which are partly under the care of the monitors, whilst the higher ones are more immediately under the superintendence of the master, who at the same time has his eye upon the whole school...."

---

2. *Ibid.*, page 2. Introduction.
3. *Ibid*, page 177.
4. The English language is taught in one school only, the Tamil in four; the Persian in 21; the Mahratta in 23, the Taloogoo in 226 and the Carnataka in 235.
5. A.N. Basu. Indian Education in Parliamentary Papers, Part I. p. 178–9, Asia Publishing House, Calcutta, 1952.

Formal Teacher-Training Programme — Early 19th Century

It is evident that hardly any formal teacher training programme was in vogue in the country till the first decade of the nineteenth century. Any government measure in this regard was a far cry. The indigenous monitorial system, however, had certain advantages. Under the direct guidance and supervision of the master, the monitors who were the selected and more capable scholars got a chance to learn class control, class management, school organisation and teaching. The organisation of the programme was somewhat like this:—

"Having attained a thorough knowledge of the letters, the scholars next learns to write the compounds, or the manner of embodying the symbols of the vowels in the consonants, and the formation of syllables, etc. then the names of men, villages, and animals, etc., and lastly arithmetical signs. He then commits to memory an addition table and counts from 1 to 100, he afterwards writes easy sums in addition and substraction of money, multiplication and the reduction of money, measures, etc. Here great pains are taken with the scholars in teaching him the fractions of an integer, which descend, not by tens as in our decimal fractions, but by fours, and are carried to a great extent. In order that these fractions together with the arithmetical tables in addition, multiplication, and the threefold measures of capacity, weight and extent, may be rendered quite familiar to the minds of the scholars, they are made to stand up twice a day in rows, and repeat the whole after one of the monitors."

Besides this, the monitors got their tuition from their masters who could, at best check, their learning on both the 'content' and 'practice' aspects. This was surely an advantage for the would-be-teachers.

The third benefit of the overall system is outlined again in the following paragraph— "The economy with which children are taught to write in the native schools, and the system by which the more advanced scholars are caused to teach the less advanced, and at the same time to confirm their own knowledge is certainly admirable, and well deserved the imitation it has received in England. The chief defects in the native schools are the nature of the books and learning taught, and the want of competent masters." (p. 181)

The trace of early form of teacher preparation as found in the monitorial system was, as one could perceive, only a drop in the ocean of need for better education. In spirit if it was laudable, in form it was beset with numerous defects. It was considered imperfect in those days as there were few persons who possessed the means to avail themselves of the advantages of general education even. This was ascribed to the gradual but general impoverishment of the country. As Campbell wrote, "In many villages where formerly there were schools, now only a few children of the most opulent are taught, others being unable from poverty, to attend or to pay what is demanded." It was mostly because of the deteriorating economic conditions in the country under the foreign rule that hurled a heavy blow to the spread of education. This is inferred from the following para again. "The means of the manufacturing classes have been of late years greatly diminished by the introduction of our European manufactures in lieu of the Indian cotton fabrics. The removal of many of our troops from our own territories to the distant frontiers of our newly subsidized allies has also of late years, affected the demand for grain; the transfer of the capital of the country from the native Governments and their officers, who liberally expended it in India, to Europeans, restricted by law from employing it even temporarily in India, and daily draining it from the land, has likewise tended to this effect, which has not been alleviated by a less rigid enforcement of the revenue due to the State. The greater part of the middling and lower classes of the people are now unable to defray the expenses incident upon the education of their offspring while their necessities require the assistance of their children as soon as their tender limbs are capable of the smaller labour." (p. 181–182)

As for the control and financial aspect of the existing pattern of education in the pre-British period and the treatment it received from the foreign rule, there was ample proof to show that "considerable alienations of revenue which formerly did honour to the State, by upholding and encouraging learning have deteriorated under our rule into the means of supporting ignorance." The practice that supported continuance and growth of learning in India had been very superbly noted as follows, "There is no doubt, that in former times, especially under the Hindoo Governments, very large grants, both in money and in land, were issued for the support of learning.... Though it did not consist with the dignity of learning to receive from her votaries hire, it has always in India been deemed the duty of Government to evince to her the highest respect, and to grant to her those emoluments which she could not, consistently with her character, receive from other sources.... They (emoluments) all purport to flow from the free bounty of the ruling power merely to aid the maintenance of some holy or learned man, or to secure his prayers for the State. But they were almost universally granted to learned or religious persons, who maintained a school for one or more of the sciences and taught therein gratuitously." (p. 182, para 22)

It is inferred, therefore, that the growth of teacher education was hardly given any attention by the foreign rulers uptil the end of the eighteenth century. While some liberal minded officers did portray the true picture of gradual decline of the indigenous education system in parts of the country in a bid to pray for some gratuitous grant for the cause of education the total assessment of the result of such efforts was one of exploitation, disregard and indifference to allow educational efforts to continue.

Primary Teacher-Training

It is not unlikely that in the late eighteenth century foreign missionaries had started in the country a few teacher training institutes essentially for the primary grade teachers. The first school worthy of mention was the normal school set up at Serampore (Bengal) where mostly teachers of the first stage of education (Primary) got training in studies in vernacular. For the first time State hands were felt in the control of education. A combination of indigenous and foreign elements was perceived. But the spirit of the existing indigenous pattern was seen gradually dying out. The monitorial system in vogue since ancient time till the end of eighteenth century was seen getting the favour of the rulers so much that the Britishers favoured its adoption in England. The same system was recommended to India for adoption in the presidencies and came to be called the Bell-Lancaster system after the name of Dr. Andrew Bell. In Madras, Sir Thomas Munro, the Governor of that Presidency held that no progress could be made by that province "without a body of better instructed teachers than we have at present."[6]

The Calcutta School Society combined arrangements for giving elementary education with that of elementary teacher education for indigenous schools. In short, the system of primary teacher's training started and developed in this country as in England from the monitorial and pupil teacher plans from 1823 onwards till 1854. The important features during this period were (i) that the training of a class of teachers would provide for the eventual extension of improved education of the natives and hence of utmost importance; (ii) that a selected group of youth should acquire specialisation in teaching; (iii) that the would-be-teacher recruits be granted a stipend out of which a small payment would be made to the masters of the school for their extra tuition to the trainees out of the school hour; (iv) that the selection and appointment of trained teachers might be done by a committee of learned Indians on the extent of their qualifications; (v) that the training consisted mainly of working through more thorough content and sending out masters with enough of practice teaching experience; (vi) that on the completion of training if proved worthy, the trainees would be awarded certificates and arrangement made for their employment as school masters; and (vii) that 'this system should be carried out both in the government colleges and schools, by grants-in-aid in all institutions brought under government inspection."[7] Thus started the practice of normal schools all over country.

The desirability of knowledge of English and western sciences grew so as to emphasise the need of graduation which eventually would imply intensive study and knowledge of the two branches mentioned above. Such graduates if and when employed in high school used to get thorough grounding from headmasters into the art of teaching. At last the modern connotation of secondary education came into vogue, although those secondary schools were largely the English teaching schools. Evidently the courses of study prescribed followed the English model more than the indigenous one.

---

6. Selection from Educational Records, Vol. I, (Bureau of Education, India), p. 74.
7. Woods Education Despatch, 1854, Paras 67-68.

Secondary Teacher-Training

Quite significant during this period is the setting up of a very few training colleges for secondary teachers and a very large number of normal schools as training institutes for primary and middle teachers. But the eternal controversy over the relative importance of general education versus training in pedagogy grew out of proportion. The efficiency was judged more from the knowledge of the course content rather than the methodology of teaching. In fact courses in methodology were yet to be drawn up.

It was for the first time that the Indian Education Commission, known as the Hunter Commission, was directed to enquire into the quality and character of the instructions imparted in schools for secondary education. Within this term of reference as stated above, the Commission had to emphasise the importance of teacher training. Suggestions were made regarding (i) the institution of a system of examination into the principles and practice of teaching required for qualifying in the teacher training course; (ii) the selection of candidates (graduates and undergraduates) for such courses of study; (iii) the duration of two types of courses for the two different groups desirous of taking training; and (iv) condition of employment in a secondary school.

Felt Need — Professional Training

For the first time in the history of teacher training in the country inclusion of studies like 'principles' of teaching was talked about and felt 'needed' for teacher preparation. Incidently prerequisites of professional training were ushered in, a knowledge about these principles was considered necessary for teacher education and the prevalent notion regarding mastery over the matter to be taught underwent a rapid change. Depending on this basic issue of the need for 'principles' practice of teaching received importance. So also was the need to look into and assess the quality and character of teachers under preparation, by evolving the fresh system of examination for those completing the teacher training course. It would naturally follow that the teacher recruitment policy of the Government got framed afresh. It became necessary to hold a 'teacher's certificate' to be made permanent in the teacher's job in a school, although the 'teacher's certificate' was not imperative for any person desirous of initial employment in a school. The lacuna that existed in this policy, did not debar a person from getting into a teacher's job — but he had to be declared professionally qualified to be made permanent in that job. Thus for a 'quality' service professional preparation with knowledge of principles and practice of teaching became an absolute condition. Upholding the recognition for mastery of matter, the Commission judiciously suggested a shorter course for a short duration for graduates and a relatively longer course for the undergraduates as the latter group needed both courses in general education as much as professional education.

There were then embedded into the Commission's recommendations, certain very valuable features.— (i) that a teacher education programme needed to be broad-based as to include rudiment of psychology, principles of class management, and the trends of educational system in vogue in a country; (ii) that a teacher was a 'better teacher' only after he had practised 'skill' in teaching; (iii) that more equipped in knowledge he is, less is the need for general education for him, and *vice-versa*. But professional education was bound to give him an additional quality in executing his responsibility so far as teaching was concerned. Over the years till today, one finds the growth and establishment of these fundamental concepts in the country's teacher education programme.

Although at certain quarters it was felt that the training course induced examination-mindedness to a great deal, it became necessary for the sake of 'quality' in education to provent all 'joy rides' in the realm of teaching. Over and above the passing of an examination, the candidate had to procure a favourable report from the school inspector as to his ability to teach. Besides, a report about his work habits and quality of performance was taken into consideration before awarding him the certificate. This brought in gradually the practice of external examination in teaching when each candidate was expected to teach a group for half an hour as a part fulfilment of his teacher's certificate. This shows that the system of assessment was quite a thorough and comprehensive one.

Quite an elaborate account of practice in pedagogic lines could be obtained from the records of Government of

India. . . . "the art of teaching is exemplified by model lessons given by the Principal and other members of the Staff, by Criticism lessons given by the students and by work in the Model Schools. Three students from Senior English, five from Junior English and five from Vernacular class are sent to the Model School every week, at the end of the week, the masters entrusted with the supervision of students send detailed criticism of every lesson and reports of their work. The criticism of lessons given by the students are designed to show how courses of lessons should be drawn up, how typical lessons in each subject be given by the student and how the principles laid down in the lectures on Education are applied in actual school work."[8]

Forms of Teacher-Training

The close of the nineteenth century saw numerous experiments in diverse directions in the field of curricular changes all over the country. A clear cut distinction also emerged as to the pattern of teacher training directed to the preparation of Primary, Secondary and Collegiate courses. The three categories of courses stood on distinctions about grade of instruction, as well as medium by which instruction was imparted (Primary essentially through vernacular medium, and Collegiate through English Medium). Even the last decade saw the institution of training courses for kindergarten teachers. While the grade-wise distinction in the teacher preparation programme took shape, prominency was being given to teachers having gone through professional and pedagogical courses of studies. Need for pedagogy got firmly established as some very practical type of learning matter, such as, Art, Agriculture, Industrial Arts, Architecture, Woodcraft, Metal Work to name a few only came to be included in the teacher training course.

In a general climate of satisfaction with the progress of teacher education all over uptil the end of nineteenth century, the Government of India's Resolution on Educational Policy (1904) expressed the need of reaffirming the principles and practices brought about in 1854 and 1882 on the one hand, and also the need for further extending and devel-

---

8. Government of India, Third Quinquennial Review, Vol. I, p. 240

oping those in response to the changing times of the country, on the other.

The toning up of educational improvements all round constituted the main recommendations of the Policy. It observed, "if the teaching in secondary schools is to be raised to a higher level,. . . . it is most necessary that the teachers should themselves be trained in the art of teaching." It affirmed that the Government of India were glad to know that local governments also realised the importance of having secondary teachers trained in the best possible manner. Referring to some teacher training institutions, the Policy stated, "these institutions have done good work, and the time has come to extend the system to the provinces where it does not exist,. . . . and to endeavour to create a supply of trained teachers which shall be adequate to the needs of the secondary schools, throughout the country. Not only must the supply be increased but the quality of the training given must be improved."[9]

The specific recommendations can be enlisted as follows: (i) that more men of ability and experience in the work of higher training will be needed, (ii) that the Training College should necessarily be equipped with great skill and abilities of capable hands, (iii) that except for graduates, the period of training should be for two years, (iv) that the graduates should have a course of instruction directed towards acquiring knowledge of principles which underlie the art of teaching as also they should acquire some degree of technical skills in the practice of that art, (v) that the course for graduates should culminate in a University degree/diploma, for others the course should mean extension, co-ordination and revision of their general studies, (vi) that the scheme of instruction should be determined by the authorities of Training College and by the Education Department, (vii) that the examination should be controlled by the same authorities, (viii) that the teaching should be closely associated with its practice and for this purpose good practising schools should be attached to each college, (ix) that the practising school should be fully equipped with well trained teachers, (x) that the students should see examples of best teaching as they

9. Indian Educational Policy. Resolution of the Government of India, Calcutta Office of the Superintendent, Government Printing, India, 1904. Para 38.

should learn teaching under able guidance and supervision, (xi) that a good library, a museum, in which samples, models, illustrations and records should be exhibited amply should go to the making of a good training college, (xii) that a proper connection be maintained between the Training College and the schools so that the students on leaving the College and entering upon his career as a teacher may not neglect to practise the methods which he has been taught, and may not (as sometimes happens) be prevented from doing so and forced to fall into the line with the more mechanical methods of his untrained colleagues, and (xiii) that old students of training colleges should be occasionally brought together again and the inspecting staff should cooperate with the Training College authorities in seeing that the influence of the college makes itself felt in schools.

No wonder that the resolutions intended to improve the quality of training for teachers. If the inclusion of the knowledge of principles of teaching was given due importance in the two earlier resolutions, the present one did justice to the practising of the skill of teaching in the light of those principles. There is hardly any aspect of 'practice teaching' that the Policy did not refer to. Right from the placement of student-trainees in the Training College and the schools for practice, uptil the assessment of his skill in teaching, — all aspects, such as, demonstration lesson, supervision of teaching, criticism lesson, impact of training to be carried over to the professional life, exchange and consequent development of fresh ideas, and skills necessary for quality teaching, inservice education and measures for constant professional growth — were mentioned, — all with a view to improving the quality of teachers. Enough stress had been laid on maintaining a live contact between the training college and the school so that on leaving college a teacher may not neglect to practice the methods which have been taught.

Comprehensive Teacher Training

In subsequent years a renewed effort was seen being made all over the country in the spread of teacher training. The professional course got due encouragement as it resulted in the award of university degree in teaching. Courses of study got revised. In some provinces it was sought that the trainees be seen in their day to day performance and the process of 'internal assessment' be introduced as the teachers and the head of the institution could only help a close supervision over the trainees. Similarly the practice in arranging refresher's courses for teachers in-service came in vogue.

How the model of a teacher training institution got shaped into a somewhat satisfactory centre of teacher education could be assessed from a report about David Hare Training College, Calcutta.

"The aim of the training course is to give the teacher an all-round preparation for his work, both from theoretical and practical points of view. On the one hand, he needs a knowledge of the subjects which he has to teach, an acquaintance with the nature of the pupils' mind and of the principles which underlie the teaching art and some knowledge of the history of education in the past. On the other hand, he learns by actual practice in the school room to control and teach his class. The theoretical training has been imparted by means of lectures on the theory and practice of teaching in relation to mental and moral science, on the methods of teaching school subjects, of maintaining discipline and on the history of education. Weekly essays on appropriate subjects have been written by the students and the library as an aid has been at their disposal, also test papers are periodically set by members of the staff. As to the practical training, each student attends demonstration lesson by staff; each has to prepare and give under supervision lessons in the schools, and each has to watch and criticise lessons given by the other student."[10]

Inherent Weaknesses in Teacher Training

The Government of India Resolution on Educational Policy (1913) pointed out once again the inadequacy of the teaching staff and the training facilities. It declared that 'under modern system of education, no teacher should be allowed to teach without a certificate that he is qualified to do so, Further the local Government should examine their schemes for

10. Government of India; Sixth Quinquennial Review. Vol. I, p. 193

training teachers of all grades, so as to provide for the great expansion.[11]

The Policy resolution highlighted some significant features as well — (i) free interchange of ideas on the success or failure of experiments is desirable, (ii) the size and working of a practising school and that of a model demonstration school should be determined, (iii) equally important is to determine the most suitable methods of procedure in practical work, (iv) the relative importance of methodology and of psychological study nevertheless should receive attention, (v) inclusion or omission of a course of study — be it of a theoretical or practical nature and uniformity of conditions governing the award of degree — all these need to be discussed by people after constant consultation, visits, conference and exchange of any experimental results. No doubt this helped in removing to a great extent the mystifying uncertainties that clouded the teacher education programmes in the country.

The ultimate effect was that between 1904–1921, the number of training colleges rose from 6 to 13 and proportion of trained teachers to the untrained increased appreciably.

Dynamic Changes Suggested

The Calcutta University Commission[12] of 1917 under the Chairmanship of Sir Michael Sadler made certain important recommendations regarding several issues of teacher education. The recommendations although were based on the working of the Calcutta and Dacca Universities, were so comprehensive as to be considered suitable for the whole country.

Exclusively, on teacher education the Commission commented on a wide range of issues, say (i) administration and academic position and hierarchies of departments, (ii) differential competencies in degree and diploma awarded by such departments, (iii) the issue of establishment, management and control of demonstration and practising schools, (iv) the

11. Educational Policy of the Government of India. Resolution of the Government of India in the Department of Education, dated 21st Feb. 1913 — Paras 51–52.
12. Government of India, Report of the Calcutta University Commission, Vol. V, Calcutta, Government Printing, 1919, p. 328–330.

need of and justification for equipping the teacher training departments and institutions on modern lines — all these came for thorough examination that brought forth valuable suggestions.

The Commission recommended the increase in the output of trained teachers as well as creation of Department of education in the University of Dacca and Calcutta. This was evidently a big step towards assigning a serious academic and professional role to the Discipline of Education. Surely, it raised the status of teacher education. The measure was to boost up the motivation of the teacher trainees, to infuse a deep interest in their pursuit of studies and cultivation of skills and competency as much as it cautioned against any slackness in dispensing with sincere service to the public.

The status having been raised, it called for maintenance of the same with other Disciplines of the University. It would not be wrong to see the origin of the concept of interdisciplinary approach in developing educational thoughts and researches talked about so much these days. With the setting up of Departments at the University, academic posts of high rank were recommended. The Commission observed, "The Department of Education should also avail of opportunities to consult and collaborate with Departments of Experimental Psychology, Philosophy, History and Economics."[13]

There was enough reason to recommend further that "the demonstration schools should be under the direction of the University, for practical trial of new methods of teaching new combinations of school subjects need new plans of school organisation." Such schools would serve as a laboratory for educational experiments. They should be different from the practising schools where practices in the skill of teaching and school organisation should normally have a place. Besides, the Department should be fully equipped with literature and periodicals of the national and international importance. Side by side, the Department should engage itself in the preparation of work of outstanding merit and offer opportunities for post graduate and research work. The teacher education in the country had been following the convention of getting tied up with the Board of School Education. For the first time a bold departure was envisaged by

13. *Ibid.*

the Commission by recommending that the Department of Education at the university level was expected to form a link between itself and the Boards of Education for High School and Intermediate Education. This specific recommendation it seems looked carefully into the levelling up of standard and quality of training that the teacher education programme should have. Several suggestions were made and one of them was that the Department of Education at the university should facilitate professional growth of teachers in service as also encourage progress of new educational movements whenever possible.

These aspects in the teacher education programme were clearly noted by the Commission — namely, the knowledge of the subject matter, skill in teaching and theoretical foundation of training. "But", the Commission observed, "under the existing conditions, the first is often unfulfilled, second rarely possible and third too little regarded by the University in framing its regulation."

Progress During the Four Decades (1900–1940)

In short, a review of progress during 1904–1940 highlighted the following features. (i) That the teacher training got reoriented on more progressive lines, (ii) number of training colleges and student enrolement showed a remarkable increase, (iii) refresher courses as inservice programme for teacher got started, (iv) researches in education got encouraged, (v) improved laboratories and enriched libraries were felt necessary for increasing professional efficiency, and (vi) need for providing practising schools and qualified staff was also stressed.

Vitalizing Teacher Training

On the other hand there was a deplorable dearth of trained teachers at every grade. While by 1934 thirteen out of the eighteen universities had set up Faculties of Education, a great gap was noticed between the trained teachers and the relevance of their training. Particularly, the need of rural India got to a large extent overlooked as teacher's job could hardly maintain a close relationship between education and rural life. A few committees stressed the need for diversified curriculum (for the spread of technical and vocational stream of training), of strengthening the training course of the primary level (where the number of attenders was ever increasing) of enlivening the rural schools and gearing teacher training to that end. The committees also dealt to some extent with the need for general improvement of teacher training, their service conditions, their salary and status and improvement of working conditions and the need for establishing close relationship with the masses of people before real progress became possible.

With a view to ascertaining what would be the minimum provision required to vitalise the main fields of educational activity in the country, the Central Advisory Board of Education (C.A.B.E.) surveyed the main fields of educational activities during the post-war period in India. The report submitted under the Chairmanship of Sir John Sargent[14] categorically states, "It is for India to decide whether the time has arrived when a national system of education is a paramount necessity." For the first time there appeared in clear terms the significance and aim of education that a country should promise to its citizens, ". . .the Board believe that there are certain fundamental principles which must determine the training of the future citizens, wherever in the world he or she may happen to dwell, and they cannot conceive that any form of social or political community will ever prosper unless the importance of fostering in the rising generation such attributes as physical fitness, intelligence and integrity of character receives the fullest recognition."

To achieve this objective primarily, the Board very strongly emphasised the need for effective teacher training. It "should be pointed out, the Report states, "that the determining factor is the teacher, the particular attention is consequently invited to the standards adopted by the Board for the recruitment and training of teachers on the one hand and for their remuneration on the other."

While referring to the inadequate and insufficient training facilities in the country and also stressing the need for starting new training schools, colleges, and even university departments of education, the Report stated the following

14. Post-War Educational Development in India. Central Advisory Board of Education. Government of India Press, Simla, 1944.

academic measures — (i) suitable boys and girls should be picked out towards the end of the high school course and attracted into the teaching profession, (ii) the courses provided should be essentially practical and especially related to the needs of the schools in which trainees will subsequently serve, (iii) refresher courses are of the utmost importance, and (iv) facilities for research be provided.

The proposals regarding the courses were thoroughly practical. For Pre-Primary teacher two years, for Junior Basic (Primary) two years, for Senior Basic (Middle) three years and for non-graduates in High Schools two years and for graduates in high schools, one year after graduation. The first year of the training should be devoted to the study of general and professional subjects, supplemented by school visits, discussions and other experiences to stimulate students' interest. A considerable part should be devoted to practice teaching next — teaching to be conducted in schools accessible to the neighborhood of training institution. They held, that "teaching practice can best be done in ordinary schools since the atmosphere of model schools attached to training institutions is usually artificial."

The Committee that went into the task of considering the question of Training, Recruitment and Conditions of Service of Teachers[15] recommended a very comprehensive programme of action. Still, the scope within which the committee functioned could not highlight, except in very general terms the details of content of the training course-theory as well as practice. Effort was directed to draw up certain general guiding principles. The details of practical experiences in terms of sessional practical work and practice of teaching was at best thought to be the function concerning details subsequent to the evolution of a more or less uniform pattern of training course. However, it was a matter of great achievement that a broad outline was chalked out. The University Education Commission (1948–49)[16] did full justice to detailing the course of the training. With a view to improving upon the standard and depth of teacher training the Commission suggested among other things the following mea-

---

15. Report of the Committee of the CABE to consider the question of Training, Recruitment and Conditions of Service of Teachers. India, Manager of Publications, Delhi, Pamphlet No. 19. 1946
16. The University Education Commission.

sures: (i) courses should be remodelled, more time and weight should be given to school practice in assessing students' performance, (ii) suitable schools should be used for teaching practice, (iii) students should be encouraged to fall in line with the current school practices and make the best of it, (iv) training college staff recruitment should be from people having first hand experience of school teaching, (v) course in theory of education should be flexible and adaptable to local circumstances. The two other distinctive measures relate themselves to (i) master's course of study to be pursued after years' of teaching experience and (ii) encouraging original work by professors and teachers on an all India basis. These measures indicate that much thought was directed to the detailed and intensive suggestions regarding the improvement of practice teaching which is the crux of successful teacher training programme.

Skill in Teaching Highlighted

The Secondary Education Commission Report[17] (1952–1953) stressed once again the importance that should be attached to teaching practice in schools. The commission reiterated the utility of having a demonstration school that is a model school attached to every training institution for practical training. There should also be a number of other schools at a reasonably near distance for the same purpose. Again for the first time, stress for the training in methods of teaching at least two school subjects was brought forth. They were fully aware of the fact that the development of practical ability in a teacher should depend on two basic things of practical bias — (i) the teaching comprising lesson planning, preparation, delivery, encouragement to students for participation — in short a command of knowledge of the subject and the skill in handling it, besides observation, demonstration and criticism of lessons, and (ii) the sessional practical work including activities such as construction, and administration of scholastic tests, organisation of supervised study and students' societies, conducting library periods and maintenance of cumulative records, that support, strengthen and enrich 'teaching'. The report states while pointing out the

17. The Secondary Education Commission Report 1952–53.

broad based purpose of the practical ability — "we feel that the scope of teacher training, particularly in its practical aspect, should be broadened to include some of these activities that a student teacher will be expected to perform when he becomes a full-fledged teacher." As for assessment of a teacher's practical ability the suggestion was to introduce the practice of internal assessment supplemented whenever needed by sample test by the Board of Examiners.

Still training institutes remained deficient in character and function. Courses taught were narrow in scope, practice teaching was less than adequate to prepare personnel who would build the nation.

Closely following the recommendations of Secondary Education Commission came those related to preparation of teachers of Basic Education. The suggestions highlighted more the philosophy and objectives of such courses than the practical aspect. Only hints regarding acquainting trainees with progressive methods and techniques of teaching, and comprehensive and intelligent understanding of correlated method of teaching different aspects were given. Of the ten elaborate objectives listed down for the new trend of Basic Education in vogue till 1956, five were directed to the development of the personality both of the teacher and the taught, while five others dealt with actual craftsmanship regarding practical teaching.

In 1955, All India Council for Secondary Education was established to suggest improvement and expansion of secondary education. The Council, through its Departments of Extension Services planned to improve school practices by active participation of teachers in service.

The beginning of sixties saw several big changes in the field of teacher education — the formation of NCERT, the establishment of the four Regional Colleges of Education at Ajmer, Bhopal, Bhuvaneshwar, and Mysore, each one to run integrated four-year teacher education programme, the inception of B.Ed. Correspondence Courses to clear the backlog of secondary school teachers, and part-time M.Ed. course started in several universities.

Teacher Training — Contemporary Scene

The Regional Colleges were set up to feed the multipurpose schools as suggested by the Secondary Education Commission. They started programme of professional and general education. Late eighteenth century saw the domination of general education over professional course. Now it took more than a hundred years to see to the balancing of general education and professional courses in teacher preparation programmes. The present century is still undecided whether any balance or compromise between the general and pedagogical aspects could be worked out and if so by what means. Observations reveal that training institutions are still inadequate to meet the increasing requirements, that the usual programme of training colleges has little relation to the actual needs and difficulties of the schools, and that many teachers are unable and unwilling to follow those methods on their return to schools.

Investigations are in progress to examine the impact of training colleges in India on actual school practice. The Radhakrishnan Commission argued for improvement of relationship between practising school and training colleges and stressed that recognition and aid to schools should be granted on the merit of the part the schools play in the practical training of recruits whose services they will subsequently use.

The setting up of State Institutes of Education in different Indian States augers well as they are entrusted with the task of follow-up work of educational practice and programming after the trained teachers are turned out of the training institution and absorbed in schools. Their main functions are improvement of classroom teaching, discussion and development, research and publication.

The Indian Education Commission (1964–1966) suggested measures to utilize teacher education and the process of learning and teaching in our millions of classrooms. One of the suggestions made was, 'to make student-teaching a comprehensive internship' in which trainees would be able to observe the entire work of the school and to participate actively in all the important professional activities of a teacher, both in and out of the classroom. This would necessitate a 'systematic collaboration and cooperation' between the schools and the training institutes. One of the measures suggested was the reorganisation of a content course which would include study of fundamental concepts and their implications for the school syllabus. This should constitute a part of the text book and source material and may, therefore, engage 20% of the time in the training programme. Such subject reorganisation should be done in collaboration with specialists in various branches from departments of university. Necessarily, the orientation to new methodology and special techniques would be necessary.

On the question of integrated courses of general and professional education, in view of the fact that no conclusive data are available to ascertain the effectiveness of such integrated four- year courses and also because the time and money needed to do this would be exhorbitantly heavy, the Commission are of the opinion that one year teacher education course be strengthened for years to come. Perhaps the improved content in addition to improved techniques of teaching with greater collaboration of training institutes and schools, will solve the problem of providing efficient teachers to the schools in the country.

It has been rightly stated that the professional studies in training institutions need revision in order to lend naturalness and practicability to the practice and theory of education. Courses should avoid platitudes and things that cannot be applied to Indian situation.

Methods of teaching used in training institutes need a careful revision according to the Commission. Whatever innovations are expected to be applied in school teaching by the student-teacher, should, without fail be put to use during their training period by the teacher educators. It is expected that student trainees could be led to maturer experiences by way of reading, thinking, discussing and deliberating and ultimately presenting project work.

On student teaching, the Commission's views are worth noting. The Commission recommended the organisation of practice teaching in two phases. Initially, the teaching programme should be intermittent when the student should be oriented to the entire school situation, to the activities, the administrative set up, library, workshop and class teaching where he should observe good teaching performed by the regular teachers. Finally, the period should involve continuous block teaching for at last eight weeks. This plan is suggested with a view to bringing before the trainees the sense that he is an integral part of the school life. Only then, the

Commission views, an effective and dedicated service would emerge.

More than a century has elapsed and streams of suggestions have flown into the main current of the Secondary Education. Committees and Commissions have, after deliberations, brought out valuable recommendations for the improvement of secondary education in the country. The problems broadly fall into two categories — (i) quantitative expansion and (ii) qualitative improvement. It was comparatively an easy task to look into the expansion of secondary education. Once the need for the expansion had been felt and the required finance made available, the speedy setting up of institution suffered less in both Public and Private hands. This had resulted in a further series of deliberations at the level of State Committees with regard to control, finance, administration, building, equipments, on one hand and selection, enrollment of students as also the training, selection and recruitment of teachers to man such schools, on the other. In short, the unchecked expansion of secondary education had far outrun the qualitative improvement that could have strengthened this vital link in the whole ladder of education.

There had all along been a sickeningly depressing tone whenever the quality of secondary education was talked about. Truly, the secondary education in the pre-independence era was a privilege that the middle class normally used to enjoy, now when the opportunities are more easily available, people of all sections can utilise them unrestricted. Still the 'style' that used to ornate secondary education has been reduced to a mere 'fashion' nowadays. More and larger crowds are thronging near the portals of institutions. The dangers of such imbalance are far too many. Education which could be an end in itself formerly, is now a means to an end. Education for natural development has thrown up a new challenge to the people to equip themselves as best as possible for the numerous employment opportunities and also to contribute to the national prosperity. Unfortunately, the education that should enable the people to rise up to the occasion is somewhat weak in both 'content' and 'practice'. The curriculum, howsoever refashioned, smacks of traditionalism; the approach to the treatment of curriculum is old and stereotyped rather than novel, scientific and creative. The technique of evaluating the individuals seems to be very narrow and of limited scope. Researchers to establish the extent, nature of qualitative deficiency are long overdue.

The two last and stupendous work done by the Secondary Education Commission and Indian Education Commission showed full awareness of these qualitative deficiencies. They also did sound a warning against "ill-conceived and improperly planned reorganisation of Secondary education in the past."

What then is the need of the hour? The importance of having well qualified and dedicated teachers to energise the task of education goes without saying. The new demands on secondary school teachers in the perspective of national needs and aspirations bring forth the desirability of orienting teacher education programme on a new line. This particular aspect never came for major changes as there has been a great dearth of research investigations in this area, in this country. As a result, the experimentation with new teaching — learning techniques, which if practised by teachers from time to time, can yield change and improvement but has to a great extent been absent in the teacher training institutions. Such examination is likely to discover trends that are common and those that are uncommon and also effective to certain institutions. A further analysis will be on the question of desirability and suitability of the usual practices in addition to the ushering in and use of new and newer models.

At the administrative and organisational level we have two distinct agencies that are involved in the training of teachers for secondary schools. — (i) the Universities through their Departments of Education and (ii) the State Governments through and Government and Government aided private training colleges. There exists also a third category of institutions which are Degree Colleges but having arranged training courses for graduates merely as a class. It is admitted that a regularly established full training college offers much better opportunity to professional preparation than a mere course attached to a degree college. No doubt, the quality of training suffers and thus indirectly affects the efficiency of the teachers.

For the better administration and governance of the teacher training programme and also for surer standard of education of quality, the Study Group on Education of Secondary Teachers in India, which met in Baroda in March 1964, recommended the establishment of State Councils for Teacher Education in different States and a National Council for Teacher Education at the Centre. The Study Group enlisted the functions of such Councils as, "to prepare programmes for the development of teacher education and supervise their implementation, to set standard in teacher education, to accredit training institution and confer recognition on them, to initiate the preparation of curriculum and syllabus for training programmes and coordinate standard and training programmes."[18] The comprehensive objectives as outlined in the above lines seem to be supporting the view that the responsibility of such programming and execution should be vested on the autonomous bodies, the Councils of Education, at the same time the role of universities in giving leadership to decision making, deploying expertise to strengthen the curricular programming in fully maintained.

Over the years the dearth of trained teachers in the fields of science and technology has been felt. With the achievement of independence, the growing need of such personnel made the planners conscious of such unprecedented pressure. Hence came the four year integrated teacher training course in Universities like the Kurukshetra and the Regional Colleges of Education at Ajmer, Bhopal, Mysore and Bhuvaneshwar started under the control and management of NCERT. These are the full-fledged colleges offering both academic subject specialisation combined with professional and pedagogical courses to the post school candidates.

There is autonomy in the execution of plans and programmes but the administrative control and standard of education are the responsibility of the respective universities. Whatever be the top heavy arrangement, at the receiving end the product of such colleges must satisfy the secondary schools. These are some of the current teacher programme the country has.

What about the content and quality of the training programme! Lots of opinion on the propriety of training 'Quality' personnel in one years time, are available. As a parallel

---

18. Report of the Study Group on Education of Secondary Teachers in India, Baroda; March 2–7, 1964; Delhi: All India Association of Training College, 1964. pp. 22–26.

the course of 4-year integrated training has come into being. It is believed that the latter type will strengthen subject specialisation with professional and pedagogical efficiency and this course will be in a position to supply teachers for areas not so far adequately manned as also the work in schools will be performed much better. Any conclusive picture on this account will depend on proper research.

Teaching being an art, the skill of teaching depends on the practice in doing teaching. Different patterns in organising practice teaching exist in the country, different methods of assessment also are in vogue. An examination into the working of several training colleges in the country, has revealed some very interesting practices prevalent in them in the post-independent era.

2

Types of Training Programmes

The existing post-graduate teacher education institutions are of various types:— (i) some are university departments or university colleges of education, (ii) some are independent colleges of education, affiliated to universities (iii) others are departments of education attached to large arts and science colleges and affiliated to a university and (iv) some are independent colleges of education or education departments attached to arts/science colleges — both types of institutions being controlled by the State Department of Education (L.T. group). The first three types lead to the degree of B.Ed. and the last one prepares students for L.T.

Merely the nature of the administrative control of the training departments does not reveal the nature of training programmes that the country has. From the point of view of nature and duration of such courses there are three types of programmes prevalent in the land. The one year training course is normally taken up by graduates who at the end of the year's study are awarded the B.Ed./B.T./L.T. degree or diploma. The second variety is found in four comprehensive training colleges which are set up in four distinct regions, at Ajmer (Rajasthan), Bhopal (Madhya Pradesh), Bhuvaneswar (Orissa), and Mysore (Karnataka) and which aim at providing a four-year integrated course in teacher education to candidates after they have successfully completed their higher secondary examination. The purpose of setting up such colleges was to supply teachers to multipurpose high schools which were then gradually getting established. A unique feature of these four comprehensive teachers training colleges is the dual control exercised over them by the regional university on the one hand and the National Council of Educational Research and Training, on the other. This integrated pattern exists also in one of the Indian universities, namely, the Kurukshetra University. The third variety, the correspondence course, for Bachelor of Education which is instituted in the Regional Colleges of Education at four places mentioned above, came into vogue under the dual control of the regional local university and the NCERT. This experiment specifically was launched upon to clear the backlog of untrained teachers who were in service already. The course is run through correspondence. The candidates who get affiliated to one of these regional colleges of education study the theory part of the programme through correspondence and attend two summer schools for practical and field work.

These three varieties of teacher training programme provide the first degree course for teachers. Courses like M.A. in Education, M.Ed. and Ph.D. and also several one year diploma programmes in some specialised branches of education can be enlisted. They indicate the diverse attempts at building up a number of advanced level teacher education programmes.

One-year B.Ed. Course

The one-year training course is the usual pattern of teacher education at the secondary level in this country. The graduate in arts/science/commerce undergo the training for one academic year. The course is divided into two broad sections — Part I, the Theory and Part II, the Practical Skill in Teaching which includes Sessional Practical work also. The details of both the parts vary from college to college and weightage in the form of marks depends on the philosophy of the programme maintained by each institution. No two opinions are similar on the question of proportion of time and effort that should be devoted to the development of practical skill in teaching and theoretical foundations related to such skills. In institutions where even half and half weightage in terms of marks is given to theory and practice, it is difficult to find if such division in terms of hours of work exists. It is a common experience to find an overwhelming importance attached to theory work in such training institutions much against the philosophy of teacher preparation work. It is believed that the development of practical ability in 'teaching' is considered to be the main aim.

No doubt, practice teaching for the 'apprentice' (would be) teacher includes a few other experiences in the field of teaching besides teaching 40 to 50 lessons. These experiences are, observation of demonstration lessons given by the members of the training college staff, delivering two criticism lesson — one each in each of the two subjects of specialisation and also observation of 20 to 25 lessons given by fellow students or regular teachers in the schools. The practice of teaching may follow the pattern of intermittent teaching for two days a week for several weeks or four days teaching in a week for a few weeks in addition to a week or two of block practice teaching. The practical work related to practice teaching may include a series of activities, namely, observation of teaching, discussions of lessons, conducting experiments, gaining skill in guiding student activities, study of some class or school problems, preparation and use of teaching aids, preparation and use of tests and so on. But the missing links in the preparation of real workers perhaps are for too many. For example, the pupil teachers seldom get a chance to know and improve upon the setting of follow-up assignment, or how to check student's assignments, or plan remedial teaching. They hardly know how to deal with problem cases or special education problems. There is much to learn from attending the staff meetings, from the school/class register work, from attending P.T.A. meetings, by helping in the conduct of examination and thereupon the preparation of examination results. In other words, very few pupils under training get a chance to draw upon the spirit of professional skills and ethics from the teaching fraternity. Thus the need for devotion and conscientiousness in executing the job of a teacher is seldom stressed during practice teaching except by individual members of the staff. In some places it is not even required that the teacher under training should qualify separately in theory and practice in order to get their final award.

Correspondence Course

Coming to the pattern of teacher education through correspondence one finds that the practice started only a few years ago as the need was felt to clear the backlog of large number of untrained but experienced teachers. The minimum number of years of service required for admission into such courses varied from 3 to 5 years. The theory part is expected to be covered through intensive self study, reading correspondence lessons and answering questions through correspondence. Since they are the teachers already in service, regular class teaching in two subject areas are thoroughly checked and supervised and suggestions for improvement given. The heads of such schools or any senior teacher are deputed to do the job of supervision in accordance with the guidelines provided by the training college. For local trainees the training college staff are in the field to supervise and guide. The correspondence B.Ed. course as offered by the Central Institute of Education, Delhi, was meant only for local teachers, and has discontinued since. For such courses as offered by the Regional Colleges of Education, the system of off-campus practice teaching has been introduced. The lesson planning is expected to be very thorough, criticism lessons conducted more carefully. The assessment procedure is strictly the same as in the regular course. The contact programme in Summer Vacation covers up part of the theory through lectures, discussions, tutorials and assignments and through extensive practical work.

Four-year Integrated Course

The reason for setting up the four-year integrated course as generally cited, is the need for supplying specialist teachers in areas of science, mathematics and fields of technology. There are other advantages also. It is in this programme that one finds courses in general education, in professional education and in scholastic areas pertaining to basic subjects rather happily integrated. The prospective teacher while majoring in two school subjects develop sufficient mastery over the subject matter that he has to teach. Acquiring knowledge and treating the same with a view to teaching them with an acknowledged competence go simultaneously in such a course . . . Besides, the course in its four years duration is likely to provide sufficient opportunities to develop proper attitudes towards the profession and greater understanding of problems and processes of education in the country. Perhaps such opportunities are inadequate both in the one-year course of 10 months duration and in correspondence courses extending over to 14–15 months. Students of the desired quality and calibre are also likely to be drawn in early in their life with a decisiveness of sticking to the teaching profession. This reduces the possibility of wastage in teacher training which infests one year teacher education courses to a great extent due to the fact that a qualified and trained teacher is often found taking up a job other than teaching.

In spite of the fact that there is a good deal of internal consistency and balance among the three aspects — the content course, general education, and pedagogic expertise in a comprehensive 4-year course — such an institution is still found to be working in isolation from the other faculties of the university. The faculty of the teachers' college, by and large, has no scope to remain uptodate in the subject matter and the college, over the years, can hardly claim any expertise in this area. Therefore, the college cannot offer its help in improvement of content competence of the teachers in service. In case there is collaboration and there exists a lot of give and take between the subject matter specialist and pedagogists — there is bound to be a qualitative improvement in classroom instructions. In certain quarters an apprehension exists which states that a programme if it is predominantly methodological, and if there is little or no concern for the growth of ideas and information which are to be taught — such a programme cannot work towards a functional balance in the preparation of teachers. The United States of America have patterned the 4-year programme of teacher education in a way that the prospective secondary school teacher follows a 4-year course either in a liberal arts or science college or in a teachers' college which offer such a course leading to Bachelor of Arts or Bachelor of Science degree. Thus having had that field of specialization he may either take separately the complete pedagogic training in one year or may study a certain number of courses in 'education' or 'pedagogy' as required. There is now a general agreement that the college education of all teachers should include a substantial proportion of 'general education' course, comprising an introduction to study the art, the social studies and the sciences at the college 'level'.

The Regional Colleges of Education have balanced the trinity of content course, general education course and professional educational courses in some satisfactory way. In the first year, one finds a major portion devoted to content courses and a minor portion to general education. The content course continue, right through the four-year course. General Education course also continues in diminishing content in all four years; professional education starts with psychology in the second year and terminates with "internship" in teaching in the 4th year.

Of the nine point objectives[1] of the four year integrated course in RCEs two relate themselves to actual practice in teaching skills — (i) to undertake pilot studies and research projects in the methods of teaching, and (ii) to collaborate with other institutions in initiating and promoting improved methods and practices .... for observation and study of the teaching process, for living as a part of a school and for teaching in a classroom.

With a view to fulfilling the above two objectives, teaching practice is organised at two levels. (i) an intensive train-

---

1. (i) To develop and provide a programme of teacher education for the multipurpose schools and to prepare teachers of technical subjects, science, crafts, agriculture, commerce, home science and fine arts, (ii) To provide inservice courses for the existing teachers of the practical subjects in multipurpose schools, (iii) To provide inservice programmes and field services for teachers, supervisors and administrators concerned with the multipurpose schools in the region in which it is located, (iv) To organise and develop a model demonstration multipurpose school, (v) To function as a regional centre for programmes of inservice education and field services for secondary schools in general, (vi) To undertake pilot studies and research project in the methods of teaching, in relation to the multipurpose schools as well as the general secondary schools, (vii) To evolve and try out improved patterns of teacher education, (viii) To prepare and disseminate instructional materials for secondary schools in general and multipurpose schools in particular, (ix) To collaborate with other institutions in initiating and promoting improved methods and practices, to function as a clearing house in this regard of children, for observation and study of the teaching process, for living as a part of a school and for teaching in a classroom.

   NCERT. Plan & Programme. Regional Colleges of Education, pp. 4–5.

ing programme in the campus utilising the resources of the demonstration schools and some local schools, (ii) an internship extending from 6–8 weeks in a school as a full time student teacher participating in all activities in general and specialising in teaching in major areas. Enrichment of these two types of experiences is ensured by diverse programmes starting from attachment to a senior teacher in the school for all possible consultation and help upto pre and post internship conferences at different levels. It is hoped that the 4-year college of education will gradually become the normal pattern of teacher education in the country.

3

Philosophy of Teacher Education

Understanding Teacher's Role

The role of the teacher and education in the reconstruction of society need no fresh emphasis. The trio, the teacher, the educational system and the society — have seldom come to terms about their respective deal — both independent and mutual. No where, have the expectations been of a deeper and wider nature than in the case of educator. Again, nowhere have they been so little explicit and undefined as in the case of teachers. Quite unconsciously, the educators are made to bear the sceptre of responsibility; whether their beliefs and capabilities are commensurate with the nature and breadth of the task they are to execute remain undetermined.

A fresh trainee remarked, "I have never been conscious of having a personal philosophy. I am aware now that a teacher has to have a philosophy of his own." Teacher education courses are run in every society. That the teacher has consciously accepted his task of teaching in good and earnest faith is itself the first requirement. Only then can a teacher be a sincere and efficient worker.

A teacher is supposed to deal with explanation and exposition of matter and ideas. His job is to theorise, speculate, moralise, and discover the most 'general' as well as the 'unique' causes and principles. He is conscious of the principles of human action and conduct. He elucidates the nature of reality, elucidates values, clarifies meaning and depends largely on language and thought. He is faced with the dire need of application of philosophical principles, of criticism of processes and products of learning; still he is ready to discover that propositions are merely hypothetical, that complaints and queries over a belief grow in a never ending variety and that truth, the ultimate reality is ever enchanting, to conclude is to stop, to doubt is to hope and continue to live.

Scope of Teacher-Education

Education as an activity needs a 'process' to explain it, a 'goal' to determine its achievement and a 'doer' to perform it. 'Teacher education' therefore, should deal with the question of (i) who the performers or would-be educators are, (ii) how does one educate them (process of activity) to be teachers, (iii) what kinds of men or women should they be, and (iv) what skills, and knowledge and behaviour pattern should they be expected to develop.

The philosophy of teacher education, therefore, relates itself to the problem of pupil entrants initially but to their educative process fundamentally. The training institutions, therefore, are faced with the task of pupil selection on one hand and arranging for the education of the future educators on the other.

(1) *Who the would-be educators are*

The entrants intending to be secondary school teachers are primarily holding a university degree and are, therefore, products of liberal education centres. The values and habits of such liberal education are supposed to make the graduates emerge as 'subject specialist' at large. The admission and selection programmes in the training institutions put unhesitatingly a heavy premium on the record of attainment of the candidate. In the absence of a better scheme, the candidate's academic background is held as a steady ground to build up a variety of criteria, used for selection. The university examination result, by and large, is the single determinant of the academic standard obtained by the candidate. But the basic criterion of entrant selection, *viz.*, the examination marks do not have the means to indicate if adequate knowledge of subject field is absent in those aspirants who are rejected on the score of having obtained less marks. Hence a complacency reigns supreme in the heart of the authority in the training institutes who evolve for themselves a negative philosophy to debar many more than admit a few. Obviously, the cognitive ability of a type is being favoured more than anything else. Moreover, as teachers they are the people who will perpetuate mainly, the growth of cognitive skills in the future generation of pupils.

Of the few other testing devices, interview and group discussions have a role to play. Again in the absence of a set of proper criteria, the observable behavior traits are drawn heavily on verbal expression of the candidate. A vital aspect of detecting the desirable attitudes, that more than anything else, proves an asset in a teacher, is completely ignored. The philosophy of teacher education subserves to the maximum extent the limitations of measures adopted in training colleges. This state of affairs proves that a positive, forward-looking philosophy in teacher education is awaited. In the absence of such positive direction a compromise formula is adhered to for all practical purposes.

(2) *How does one educate them*

Coming to the second phase of the teacher education programme *viz.*, the actual process in which the education in a teacher training institution is planned and conducted, one faces two distinct streams of guiding thoughts. The one has very close adherence to and following of the pedagogical practices and the other leans heavily on the psychology of the teacher, the personality development of the would-be teacher. The Herbertian principles have, over the centuries, been the fountain of 'inspiration' for both the teacher educators and the pupil teachers. The student teacher is guided in the development in him of certain skills which should predominantly be practised in the class room. He exposes certain knowledge content in basic subjects and is believed to be helping children develop their knowledge in respective fields. His experience in following the pedagogical principles has reference mainly to the field of knowledge, practices in society outside might be at variance, children's apathy to grasp the matter which the teacher intends them to grasp need not be, it appears, a consideration to have a fresh look at the training college techniques. The benefit does not go beyond the cognitive field. Methodology is prescriptive rather than exploratory. The children, at best, can be expected to develop as the normative, 'ideal' type. Change is induced in them, when it should follow from them. Following such a chequered path, the programme in a teacher training college, can expect little innovation except from within the masters. Activities around practice of different nature are managed well in such an authoritarian domain. And schools that come under the practice teaching do only provide ground for the continuation of the '*status quo*'. Soon they cease to be reciprocal. It is the training college that needs the schools, not the schools, the training college.

Coming to the second school of supporters — it seems, psychology replaces pedagogy. Install the balanced personality, it says, as soon as possible, and the effective teaching will be taken care of. The discovery in the field of psychology emphasises that the teacher needs to know himself as much as his learners. Accordingly, psychology holds, that 'craftsmanship' can never satisfy the need of the hour. Approach the learner to discover his learning process; there is no need to dictate to him the knowledge he is supposed to receive, or the way he should receive it. The teacher's involvement will process the mechanism of learning. The teacher, under such a concept, should be a 'free' practitioner, himself 'liberated' in his own development and thus free the learner from authoritarianism into a relatively permissive atmosphere.

It appears that the teacher education centres in India, by and large, prefer a routinised academic programme than a permissive exploratory one. Tutorials, assignments, tests and internal assessment are means to sharpen the skill of teaching. No wonder, the training colleges smack of traditionalism; experimentation that should be the hall mark of change is not much encouraged. A direction to the new education that should flow from such teacher training institutions is missing, the very purpose of the existence of such centres is being rightly questioned except that the justification is sought in the perpetuation of the old order.

Looking at the schools, the philosophy of the either stream of thoughts has failed, long ago, to inspire anybody so to say. A teacher ought to have a training, is a well admitted condition. How well can the benefits of such training be put to use is a serious question. The school administration normally prefers an unquestioning worker ready to obey and oblige. Conditions of service and security, at present, do not at all relate themselves to a healthy and growing philosophy of education that might have originated in the training college and might be seen energising the practice of education at the school level. Schools seldom look upon the teachers' college for any guidance or inspiration. They are more obligated to the departments of education which look after essentially the administrative aspects of education. That the new recruits in the schools might have imbibed a fresh thinking and a new attitude to work, is seldom anybody's expectation. Immediately after the qualifying examination a new graduate of education makes the least effort to remember or to make use of the basic truths about reality, *i.e.*, the meaning of the process of education. For him a relatively undefined purpose predominates in his place of work. It is as good as unlearning the past and getting conditioned to a new set up. In rare cases, a bright spark, nurtured in the training college, and absorbed in a school, finds an existence worthy of its calibre and makes efforts to send out occasional signals to cause change and progress. Thus, even if the philosophy is likely to be present in the theory of education, its appreciation is rarely felt in the function of education.

(3) *What kinds of men and women should they be*

The present day teacher in India is hardly recognised as 'a direct linear descendant' of his illustrious forbear. Also, it is not proper to expect a too-long continuance of out-dated forms and methods. Education in ancient India was hardly a 'calling' in the true sense of the term. Still it was vested on the illustrious Brahmin teacher whose role lay singularly in the precise and objective and most detailed clarification and exposition of the sacred texts full of mystical contents. Teaching was a life-long task and not tied around specific subjects in regulated dose to be completed in specific period of time. It was the supreme duty of the 'guru' to pass on to his students all he knew of the sacred texts and from his experiences for the supreme aim of education — the knowledge of Brahman or the Absolute could not be acquired simply from literature. His relationship with his pupils was in the highest degree spiritual. The affectionate care from the one and reverential devotion from the other got established over the long period of studentship spent in the guru's house. Through this apprenticeship, during which the student performed many menial tasks even for his teacher, the student came to learn necessary powers of introspection, dedication and contemplation. A line to that effect is found in the Gita.

"तत् बिध्धि प्रणिप्रातेन परिप्रश्नेन सेवया"

'Know That by prostration, questioning, and by service to the Guru.'

On a close analysis it seems that the teaching profession was held, by common consent, very respectable. A teacher came to be associated in time, with sacrifice, personal dignity, a sense of high social responsibility, vast learning and mostly of religious frame of reference. No institution, however, was required to license a teacher either as religious head or a secular functionary. However, the ancient teacher had an established reputation of being a pious man with an outstanding scholarship mixed with unusual generosity and goodness. If the teacher worked with a missionary spirit of self sacrifice, the State and the people at large held the learned teacher and his institutions in high esteem and helped them liberally.

Further, since the teaching class mainly belonged to the brahmin community these teachers were responsible both for secular as well as religious arts and sciences. The brahminic cult which gave over to Budhistic and Jainic system for a considerable period of time retained its character somewhat throughout the period till it came back — but after having lost all its lustre. "Schools gradually became removed and cut-off from the main spring of life and the objectives of education restricted as they were, became increasingly meaningless."[1] The Muslim thinkers also maintained that to acquire the vision of the ultimate a long period of preparation is necessary. Although knowledge is obtained either through revelation or by the application of experiences and reason, the process of learning is helped by the teacher who

1. R.P. Singh, The Indian Teacher. National Publishing House, Daryaganj, Delhi-6, 1969.

is indispensable, and who treats his pupils as his own children — most humanely and compassionately. Muslim institutions in India, although depended very much on religious instructions, neither got isolated from life in society nor taught meaningless courses.

However, the purpose that education all these years was serving, lost its former ground. The standard had a fall as the exercise on education amounted to mere memorisation of sacred texts. It was neither religious nor a secular education that was in vogue in the country. It offered an excellent opportunity to the ruler class, the Britishers, to introduce a type of education that suited only their end. A new and an effective channel of communication between the British administrators and the Indians was necessary to be established. Education that they started gave the proper fill up. The band of teachers that emerged to install the new education in English language for the new 'Raj' was none else but the middle class intellectual elite who undertook to bring a system that would treat all the 'natives' on the same footing. Thus, the old and ancient mooring in the typical Indian soil was lost. The response to the new situation had got to be new. The teaching profession got a new colour. The 'secular' character became prominent, and so did the system of 'formal' payment and acceptance of salary. The very traditional practice of the priestly nature around the guru was replaced by an 'outlook towards a job' merely. Thus teaching became a transactable commodity to be valued on a commercial term. The occupational group of teachers might be seen as having one of the largest following today in the nation's professions. The task of preparation of such professional members is to be taken seriously.

It is acceptable that a modern teacher is recognisable more as a counterpart of his western ally in the same profession rather than as a mantle bearer of the traditions of the great gurus of the land. It is essential for the teacher educators to be conscious of this characteristic drift of the Indian teacher into the twentieth century existence. Due to the non-availability of any indigenous criteria to evaluate the professional expertise in teaching, the western model is often taken help of to do the job. All our surveys and conferences conducted so far by teacher education departments reveal to have never made an honest attempt to signify and outline the criteria to evaluate teaching.

Hence the notion has remained vaguely in the mind of the members who are entrusted to both prepare and evaluate the recruit in the line. Considering the need for such a profitable exercise, the sociological standpoint would without doubt justify a 'differential concept and criteria' to evaluate an Indian teacher. So long as this hunch for relative differences among members of the same profession but belonging to the different culture complex is not proved unnecessary, it is affirmed that our pattern of teacher education is not established on a sound footing yet.

The impact of such instability can be unfortunate and far reaching. The teacher education philosophy in the changing world needs to be far more dynamic in order to be effective. The late twentieth century is marked, as much by tremendous explosion of knowledge as explosion of aspirations. In a developing nation where political independence is newly achieved, the aspirations are far outstripping the existing resources and growth of manpower and material benefits. The difficulties of an already formidable task of development are accentuated when stable policies are yet to be framed, standard of behaviour yet to strike a desirable and profitable level leading the nation ultimately to achieving a 'style of life'. It is to these ends that education should gear its machinery to quick and qualitative improvements. A man in the teaching profession has to function as a multiphasic personality. The challenges to the would-be teacher are manifold. He has to outgrow his boundary at a galloping speed. His literacy is not merely an acquaintance with 'letters' but with invention in every field, with industrial power, with medical science, with mass media and with highly developed scientific knowledge. Men and women who are wanting to join the training college, need to do a heart searching in respect of (i) their aspirations, (ii) capabilities to meet new economic, in tellectual and political situations both national and international, (iii) the background that might have been a constant battle against deprivation of all kinds and yet (iv) their confidence and an iron will to usher in a change for the better. Philosophy of teacher education is not in the sources of academics, nor in the pedagogy of the profession alone but in the deeper attitudes to work relentlessly to serve the underprivileged and to create a better environment from time to time. In the plane of Indian educational system, the clarion call to this effect is still awaited.

(4) *What are they expected to develop*

Originally the job of a teacher was never viewed to deal with mundane matters. The pillars to pass on the special knowledge of a society from one generation to the next were the priest, the physician, the lawgiver and the teacher. The teacher was thought to be divinely inspired — one who knew the truths and realities of life and death, about the seasons and the movements of planets, and the universe and who was the agent to bring forth the vision of divine truths, if need be. Teacher's role was to transmit a kind of wisdom that he could cultivate even by keeping himself cut off from the company of men and society. The attributes he possessed were those of an 'ideal' human being, he was the benefactor of mankind, and his words directed the events of life. Later periods found him taking over from the religious priests the task of being the conserver of traditions. The secular functions got more importance undoubtedly. Hence the 'ideal' in him soon faded into a vague reality-undefinable. It was not difficult to recognise him taking prominent role in such field of knowledge which guided practical day-to-day organisation of the society. The image of a teacher through the ages has been aptly portrayed in the following words. "Plato's philosopher teacher was nevertheless useful. With access to the supreme good, through the study of dialectic his exact knowledge of ethics and metaphysics enabled the philosopher to concoct suitable myths which would instill in the masses self-control and obedience to their rulers."[2] The poet teacher was attacked by Plato as an unreliable source of knowledge whereas the rhetoric teacher with his command of style and diction prepared his students for democratic institutions in Athens. China believed in morality as the way of life in a teacher. In their view the exampler teacher, among other virtues, should be benevolent, humble, gentle towards all accepting and fulfilling obligations and responsibilities. In Rome, on the other hand, the tyrant-teacher would drive the student on, by cane and whip. Again Sophists were teachers who catered to the interests of their students. Use of skills such as logic; rhetoric and dialectic grew up. Gradually the

2. G.Z.F. Bereday & J.A. Lauwerys, The Education and Training of Teachers. The Year Book of Education, 1963, Evans Brothers Limited, London.

eighteenth century saw the birth of National Systems of Education in several western countries. Therefore, down the ages, the skills and abilities of a teacher have changed a great deal. Today the need for universal education is evidently a secular need and the latter is continuously changing. The teachers' lot is bound to change and so are his skills and abilities on one hand and the application of the same on the other.

The view of the purpose of education a country holds eventually helps to determine the concept of the desirable teacher, his role and goals. In other words, the views on what teachers should know, how they should be recruited, and professionally prepared are perpetual worries in human mind. The various reports and reviews on Indian teacher education deal mainly with two aspects *viz.*, control of teacher education institutions and content of their courses. The differences in nature and extent of the control (be it private or university or State governed) do not unfortunately indicate any sharp and significant differences in the programming of such training courses. The control has been diverse but not so the programme. Consequently, the concept of skills and abilities that a teacher should develop to suit the changing needs of the socio-economic set up of the country has not undergone any vital change.

Anxiety has been experienced and expressed but less has been achieved in the direction of formulating a new philosophy of teacher preparation course. Quoting a pre-independent document[3] 'one finds the anxiety for a breakthrough so well recorded,'. . . the Committee Reports provide the foundations upon which an efficient system of public instruction suited to the needs and circumstances of their country — can effectively be erected. . . . It will be for the responsible educational authorities to devise for themselves, within the general lines laid down, the type of education most appropriate to their particular areas and with this object in view, to give the fullest encouragement to every form of potentially useful experiment. While the aim throughout has been to devise a system which is essentially Indian, the Board at the same time believe that there are certain fundamental principles

3. Post War Educational Development in India. Report of the C.A.B.E., January, 1944.

which must determine the training of the future citizen.... training of the intellect and the training of the character must proceed side by side. There is then a broad hint to suit educational development to local needs and that the existing teacher training institutes should prepare teachers with that aim in view.

The Indian University Education Commission (1948–49) remarked, "There is not much of variation between the courses prescribed in the different institutions."[4] Should the guiding philosophy precede or follow the practices? While inaugurating the first meeting of the committee appointed by the Indian Ministry of Education to revise the existing B.Ed. syllabus, in 1956, Aug. 7, K.G. Saiyidain, the then Educational Adviser, pinpointed two basic features to be borne in mind.

(1) Whatever knowledge is imparted to the trainees should have a direct bearing on the day-to-day school problems.

(2) It should be the endeavour of every teacher in a training college to link up his theoretical work with the new socio-economic forces that are operative in the national life. Unless that is done, the training will lose much of its significance and the trainee will find it difficult to develop a complete and coherent picture of life.[5]

No doubt the statements point out two essential objectives of teacher education for the present Indian context. It was suggested that the educational objectives be deduced from the prevailing broad sociological framework which education should serve ultimately. But specific objectives remained rather untouched because policies about teacher training could not be suitably decided upon. The implications of such objectives are well worth probing. The matter of study in the training colleges then, as one infers, should be practical and child life oriented. Themes should emerge from day to day life in a school, activities planned around the school, child's needs, where the child is the pivot of all care and attention, where he and the environment around him should direct learning rather than theories from books be imposed

4. Indian University Education Commission, 1948-49.
5. Secondary Education, Ministry of Education, Oct. 1956, p. 9.

on an imaginary learner. such state of affairs does not obtain in training colleges in India today. Not even the climate permits any proper and thorough experimentation on or application of already existent theories-principles of education. To be optimistic, possibilities of creating new postulates and theories will not be a remote dream. The teachers under training if given a little encouragement, could be an eager lot of people having a desire to explore avenues, to establish facts, to experiment in a new light and to promote and direct the learning of the young child. The skills and abilities of the pupil teacher will not be seen developing in a caged condition where they feel cramped by not getting a chance to see and prove what they want to see and prove, but what they are asked by the authorities to see and find out. Given that freedom and scope the abilities of pupil teachers in actual operation may show tremendous change. A combination of theory and practice to lead on to a fresh innovation where the progressive elements will be in sight is highly desirable at the moment. The problem in India is rather a special one. The traditions of the ancient past are looming large on any present day practice. Since teaching is one of the very ancient arts in India, the tendency to continue with a part of the ancient model exists very much in the day to day practice of the teacher training institutions. At least the ideals are preached quite often. This is not to mean that the nation is ever conceiving of a time when it will severe all ties with the past. The ideals to be retained have got to be checked against the conditions current in modern times. A very big gap then has got to be bridged and for that, the fresh minds of the younger generation have got to be mobilized to lead the affairs of the nation. What would satisfy us — a newly varnished old furniture or a new model of a furniture altogether — is not yet clear. That India needs progress is a common slogan. The transition period is a period of anguish, a time to wait for the birth of a new age. Do the teacher educators ever tune their teaching-learning activity to this problem — the biggest ever.

The western world has got itself freed from the clergy dominated form of State Education; India has got herself freed from the Brahminic control of religio-philosophic traditions. Even on the secular plane do the societies meet and communicate about their problems and progress? Should they?

And on this decision where a new philosophy has got yet to show the way, the practices in the training colleges continue to follow a stereotyped model lacking vigour and vitality.

Should the university take upon itself the task of influencing profoundly the activities of the training college it should be in the area of academic standard, — the mastery of the subject matter fully and completely. But there is the other school of thought that upholds the interest in professional subjects. The training colleges in India, by and large, follow the latter style. At least uptil now this is the pattern followed in England.[6] For example, the basic subjects are principles of education, psychology, history of education and methods of teaching. These are such subjects which constitute the professional studies. They should help the teacher, (i) to understand his pupils, (ii) recognize social functions of the schools, (iii) to make him aware of the aims of education in his society, and (iv) to know how to teach. Through these professional courses and the practice in the classroom he will acquire best his essential qualification as a teacher. His apprenticeship courses should help him a great deal.

Teacher — Scope of the Function

Quite recently, the Committee on Plan Projects, appointed by the Government of India, in its Report on Teacher Training,[7] noted "that teacher's task today is to educate children for their physical, mental, emotional, moral, and spiritual growth and this task is to be handled by persons who are familiar with methods of teaching and certain special skills for the purpose as well as knowledge of psychology of children." For such a goal to achieve the committee suggested some specific objectives that the teacher education should: (1) enable the trainees to acquire the skills and techniques needed to teach young children, with the help of modern knowledge of child psychology and methods of teaching; (2) inculcate in the educands the ideals and accepted behaviour pattern of the society in which we live and whose purposes we serve; (3) develop in the teacher trainee certain attitudes,

6. The Education & Training of Teachers, The Year Book of Education, 1963, Ed. Bereday & Lauwerys, Evan Brothers.
7. Report on Teacher Training. Committee on Plan Projects. Government of India New Delhi, May 1964, Chapter II, p. 4.

values and interests in conformity with the ideals of democracy, and our developing economy.

Modern education aims at education of the whole person. Every teacher should have a deep knowledge and understanding of children and skill in applying that knowledge and understanding. He has to learn the job by an arduous and long practice which is possible only when his practices are built on sound theoretical knowledge. It is quite evident then that the philosophy of teacher education, in India, rests on the practice of skills supported very much by pragmatic ideals.

Case Studies

Case studies of several training colleges in India, reveal several interesting features. It has been possible to categorise the colleges into four groups depending on the theoretical policies that each group holds and tries to see the fuller implication of the same in and through their respective training programmes.

(a) The two university departments of education hold the view that the bachelor of education course is exclusively a professional educational programme and hence it should help the student trainees to become efficient and effective classroom teachers. Their competence and mastery over the respective subject content which they are going to teach is assumed once they are the graduates from the university. Yet the teacher is expected to be well informed in his field, to understand both the theory and practice of the pedagogy. He functions better in the classroom where the planning, preparation and execution of a good lesson plan would be a testimony of his command over the subject matter. A significant view held by them is that the theory oriented teacher functions better than the practice oriented one. Still the duration of the course does not offer any scope for a general and liberal education programme although they are not averse to introducing a liberalised teacher education programme. He should be an effective classroom teacher first and an educational administrator afterwards. Accordingly, the theory of pedagogy should be given more weightage in terms of marks and time. Classroom teaching and sessional work should be considered mutually complementary, although of the two, the classroom teaching should receive more importance than sessional practical work.

(b) The Regional Colleges of Education are the comprehensive Teachers' Colleges with several provisions of teachers' training course — *viz.*, one year, four-year integrated, and several diploma courses in special subjects. For each type, the authorities postulated varying philosophical bases. The focus is highly on the development of teacher's personality and professional competence. The teacher preparation programme should build up on a foundation of general education with experiences in specialised academic plus professional preparation. The general education contributes to the growth as a person, special academic education provides scholarly knowledge and thorough mastery of the subject to be taught, and professional education leads to understanding and skill in professional performance. The aspect of pedagogy should essentially evolve round, (i) psychology in general, (ii) psychology of the child and the learning theory in particular, besides, (iii) values and historical perspective of education as a profession.

The one year course and the four-year course each stands on different footing. The one year course aims at producing effective classroom teachers in special subject areas. There is no emphasis on instruction in general education, nor is there any on advanced level content courses. The entrant requirements explain the reason that the one year course students join teacher education programme after completing their graduation, whereas, the four-year course people come after completing the secondary education. However, some programme of instructions and examinations in the subject-content area in one year course is already there. It is not a very thorough one. Still it provides for (i) orientation to the latest developments in the content field, (ii) acquaintance with new researches in the field and (iii) scope for adjustment of the pupil teacher's knowledge of the subject to the needs of school children. The colleges feel that the 4-year integrated course certainly offers a better scope for liberal and integrated programme of teacher education by involving all three essential parts — *viz.*, general education, content and professional courses.

Lot of emphasis is given on teaching as a practice of skill. The colleges believe that teaching is a skill, the art in teaching can develop by continuous and long-drawn guidance and supervision in an internship situation. A wholesome teacher education programme should be woven round a framework of theory on one hand and practical work related to pedagogy on the other. Since practice in teaching is more important and useful, the emphasis on theory should be relatively less and hence the ratio of weightage between practice and theory is 60:40. The colleges do express a sort of dissatisfaction about the insistence by some universities on more weightage to the theory work. In their view theory should move around the methodology of teaching rather than around bases like philosophical, sociological, psychological, and historical. Sessional practical work of all varieties — such as, assignments, field work, laboratory study, test administration, study of the problem child, and cumulative record card, preparation of teaching aids — should be treated as activities supporting and strengthening the skill in teaching, and not as activities important in themselves. They need not be there only for the sake of having them or loosely connected to the training course. Hence it should receive much less weightage than the practice of teaching.

(c) In the third category of teachers' colleges fall a variety of institutions which, (i) offer 1-year B.Ed. course, (ii) are established with an aim of preparing teachers in a special branch, (iii) are affiliated directly to the university for the purposes of academic and administrative governance. The colleges hold the view that B.Ed. is a professional course intending to prepare good classroom teachers. There is a special and serious emphasis felt in all these colleges for teachers receiving practical orientation primarily during their training course. Good command over the subject matter, is the first essential requisite for the teacher according to them. They are rather dismayed to find out that B.Ed. students with good standing in the university degree or post graduation in Arts/Science/Commerce lack in subject matter knowledge. It is necessary, in their opinion to have understanding in fundamental concepts but university education might be equipping them to acquire only extensive knowledge of the subject than the fundamentals of concepts. Thus they feel that teachers' colleges should do something to improve on content knowledge.This will benefit the school children immensely. But 'content teaching' in the training college should be restricted to the elucidation and clarification of the fundamental and basic concepts. This can have a place only as a compensation for the lack of competence in the subject area but not as a regular feature. Teacher preparation programme should include theory and practice of pedagogy wherein greater emphasis in terms of marks and time spent should be on the practical aspect, more so on the teaching practice. One of the colleges, goes to the extent of including industrial crafts, mechanical farming, textile and electrical engineering, etc. in their content of instructional programme. This view as held by the college has received support from the university to which the college is affiliated. Located in an industrial estate the college ensures all importance to such crafts which fetch a large student clientele likely to be benefited by such courses on one hand and by getting avenues of employment on the other. All the colleges, however, hold that sessional work — as part of the requirement of B.Ed. is to be related to the needs of the entire school programme and to producing effective teachers.

(d) The colleges of education that belong to the fourth category hold emphatically that teaching is a skill, and can be acquired and perfected by a long-drawn period of supervised practice-in-teaching. As such classroom teaching should receive the maximum emphasis in a one-year teacher training course. The impact of it should be seen in attaching more emphasis in teaching in terms of marks and time devoted than for either 'theory' work or 'sessional' work. The colleges never approve of liberalised teacher education programme. A distinctive characteristic of colleges of this category is seen in two of the features, namely, (i) they emphasise more on rigorous part of 'training' than on liberal aspect of 'education', (ii) since academically advanced and relatively meritorious candidates are selected for the course, the question of teaching the content subject is immaterial. What is important is the practical aspect of teaching; for developing such skills application of pedagogic principles in classroom situations is what is necessary. Hence for the teacher trainees an advanced level subject content in the training college has no place. Rather the knowledge of such subjects should be adjusted to the needs of the secondary school children. In one case, a rarity indeed, the college does not expect any sessional practical work from the trainees.

Thus from the above review, several features emerge: (i) That the philosophy of teacher education has not been showing a uniform trend in this country. (ii) That wherever 'education' is treated as an academic discipline, the theory of education has received relatively greater importance, this is the pattern seen in the university department of education; (iii) Wherever 'training' is treated as more essential for professional preparation it is pedagogical principles around long practice-teaching that has received importance; (iv) Except in 4-year comprehensive teacher training institutions, the need for 'subject content' education is less felt; (v) The assumption that the teacher trainee is already a 'master' in his subject is commonly held, though not proved; (vi) 'Skill' in teaching is considered more important in training institutes in contrast to 'personality' and 'competence' aspect in department of education; (vii) Practical aspect in teaching for an efficient classroom teacher is never missed sight of by any one, hence this aspect should have weightage 'equal' if not more to the theoretical grounding. So far as this study reveals, there is hardly any chance of teaching ushering in a new era of social change. The teacher training colleges, under review, seem to be ready to serve as a faithful servant; there is, however, a slight hope that university departments of education may play the role of the harbinger of new and relevant theory of education that would suit the coming generation of the 21st century.

4

Policies and Practices of Admission To Teacher Education Courses

In any discussion on the selection of proper personnel for a task, it is relevant to question! 'What is the nature of the task', 'What type of personnel does the task need', 'What measures should ensure the best selection of such personnel before the training scheme is launched upon; and 'How are the personnel trained for the job.' The problem posed above requires a thorough job-analysis of the task on one hand and a critical and careful venture in examining the selection and training of people on the other.

Nature of the Work

In considering the case of 'teaching', as a job, the analysis has baffled many educators, since 'teaching' is so individual an activity and so profound a task. The teacher might have obtained his education either in the university or a college of education, or in a department of education of a college of liberal arts; but the way he proves his worth in the task he has to perform, testifies the worth not so much of the centres of training, but his own individual education. To a great measure it depends upon what the individual brings from within himself to the educational process. By this criterion a non-graduate teacher may sometimes show excellent performance whereas the university graduate teacher may stand for a poor show.

Type of Worker the Task Needs

The question of selection of trainee teachers touches upon two issues — (i) people desirous of entering into the field, and (ii) people weighing the desirability of having such people join the field. It leads to a golden combination when the desirous and the desired join. The desirous ones may either be prompted by conditions like aptitude and ability on their part or conditions of a personal self-seeking nature which do not warrant the furtherance of any benefit to the job. Both these two types throng the doors of the teacher training institutes trying their luck. It is now the responsibility of the training college to put up before the candidates the multiple devices of testing to screen the ones it can call 'the most able' and 'desired' for the field. When the regular turnouts do not prove very successful as teachers, the training colleges and the methods of training them come for rigorous criticism. Even the very process of selection of candidates stands condemned and fresh demands are made to change the procedure of selection. It appears then that the question of selection procedure is never an isolated item, rather it is a matter very closely linked up with the objectives of teacher education.

Let us look at the problem from another angle. Those who are approaching the selection tests are experiencing a trauma in view of the fact that the objectives of the very course are not at all clear to them. For them selection or no selection is a game of chance. The purposes of selection and for that matter the purpose of the various measures of selection have not been spelt out to them. Could it be suggested that there be some specific document developed (in matters of vocational guidance) which would orientate the group desirous of joining training during their pre-training period to the pre-requisite conditions that go with the job of a teacher. A bit of heart searching will be there on the part of all candidates with a view to understanding their own mind, capabilities and aptitude much before they appear before the selection period. Incidentally, the objectives of teacher education will receive emphasis when the pre-requisites are spelt out in common terms. However, the reluctant and casual second grade candidates who might have drifted into the course may give a second thought before they approach the portals of the teacher training institutes. Several hazards thus will be avoided and a good selection will be ensured. This even at the initial stage, can stop the number of candidates swelling year after year from appearing for admission tests, and a more purposeful selection in a worthwhile manner will not be difficult.

An Ideal Teacher

What then is the image of an ideal teacher? It would be generally agreed, that the first requisite is a thorough command of the subject matter to be taught — that is the knowledge of the subject matter he is going to teach when he is qualified as a teacher. This is true of all countries — a small elite — highly motivated towards learning and whose environment makes the task of teaching easier and gives their education its meaning and relevance — that is the situation in German Gymnasium. True, a breadth of knowledge is as important as its depth. He should keep himself abreast of major developments in his subject, throughout his teaching life. His mind should be kept active by a constant thrusting towards new fields of knowledge. Apart from knowledge of his subject, he should have wide interests to help the pupils in contact with him, to explore new and newer ideas of wider and varied interests. A limitless world with unlimited range of knowledge is ahead of him. It is his job to churn out the precious bit of knowledge. He should know and understand the world outside the school gates. Apart from the mastery of the course content, an opinion quite strong is voiced, and that is the importance of liberal education of teacher both here and abroad. Of the total instruction in the teacher training institution the greater part includes such basic subjects as the history and philosophy of education, and psychology and sociology. If properly taught, they can contribute as fully to the achievement of the proper goals of higher education as do other subject generally found in liberal arts curriculum. Lot of weight should be given to the statement which can offer an answer to the age-old question on the desirability of prescribing content course or liberalised education to the students under training. Moreover, the teacher educators in charge of teaching the aforesaid subjects should endeavour to satisfy the special need of the broad based curriculum, in such a manner that the effort and achievement justify the standard of the professional course as equally prestigious as the university level work of other disciplines. An objection to the effect that the method specialists in training colleges maintain less contacts in their respective subject areas with the academic disciplines at the university level will be duly met with. This will incidentally improve the standard of teaching both in the training colleges and the schools respectively. To go a step further, such courses in the training colleges will meet double requirement (i) maintaining high standard of academic discipline and (ii) placing school population on to a sound foundation and leading them to the goals of higher learning. It is proper to remember that training colleges can act as a liaison between the young and the adult learners of the society and such colleges should be the meeting ground of proper exchange and growth of learning. Never should one miss sight of the fact that the would-be-teachers under training are the torch bearers in this case. Education will gain universal recognition when there will be opportunities for greater university participation in teacher training.

A New Awareness

Thus said, only a part of the image of the teacher is reflected. In recent years the future teachers have a stupendous responsibility to be pioneers in tackling with high number of student population from a far more widely dispersed social background. They are likely to receive children in schools whose parents might not have received even a rudimentary education in three Rs. The awareness of the needs of such socially underprivileged groups is likely to develop on ground different from the available source materials of psychology and sociology. If the new teachers have to perform their task valiantly as the need of the hour would demand the curriculum should undergo a thorough and extensive process of rationalisation. The building up of 'the attitude' and the preparedness in the young blood to take to teaching as a profession under such circumstances will pose fresh problems for the teacher educators right from the selection of fresh recruits of pupil teacher to the final satisfactory preparation for the job. Subject mastery is in no way receding in the background. All the more the mode of presentation of the material learnt will be crucial. The knowledge of the learners' background, the interest to know, and their previous family background will need method of instructions which may not in near future rely exclusively on conceptual and theoretical procedures. The trend will receive special attention and application when the teacher's post training placement in rural or urban side, in industrial area or agrarian centers will be considered. Faced with the problems of teaching scientific and technical subjects to ever greater numbers of the school population, educators will be forced to evolve more efficient techniques, may be the use of teaching machines also. The educator will have to be far more cautious when he will realise his responsibility and side by side his incapability to predict the impact of true professional preparation — be the need in the area of special education or adult and social education or educational technology.

Social Responsibility of Teacher

A part of the distinguished role that the teacher plays is in the area of social responsibility. How is the teacher held by the members of the public — as a worker, and as a parent? The modern society — the society that upholds freedom for individuality is experiencing a drastic shakeup of traditional values which the teacher might be expected to defend. The modern era is witnessing a rather materialistic view of education in which the teacher is no more than a figure who can only devise techniques for passing examinations. His talents are recognised not by the education he has acquired, the knowledge he possesses but by his special ability by which he can help students to occupy worthwhile position in industrial and commercial life. The present generation swears on the promise of egalitarianism but believes sadly on a hierarchy of wage packet rather than on humane and genuine consideration that should be the base for egalitarian society. So the teacher is seldom esteemed for any of his intrinsic worth.

Teacher as a Person

'Teaching' is doing the job for its own sake, 'a mere earning a living'. If that be the situation, the teacher is inevitably affected by worldly atmosphere. But of all professional people, the teacher is expected to lay the foundations of a new culture. He has to free himself from the action of merely defending the wornout concepts and he has to show the way to usher in fruitful social change. Judged from the angle of his financial status, he is no better than skilled technicians' counterpart. But the whole array of behaviour traits that he is expected to possess point out to his quality as a human being. His influence on his fellowmen, his sense of social responsibility, his behaviour norm, his moral authority — go a long way to establish him beyond dispute — as a man of integrity and character. Hence limitations in him in any big or small measure appear unpardonable. So as a reformer, the teacher is more a man than a myth.

Teacher in the Classroom

Conceiving the teacher as a classroom expert, what are his assets? It is necessary for him to acquire an amount of knowledge and for that matter he must possess both general and special aptitudes. He must possess a retentive memory, steady attention, quickness of mind. Pedagogical abilities in him are the 'potentiality' to achieve mastery; they are not yet skills already acquired, but in the process of being acquired. Such abilities can be noted as pedagogical power of observation, imagination, tactfulness, a high sense of duty to oneself and to others, organising ability and distributive attention. It seems, therefore, that a closer examination of the teacher's work in school, his image before the public, his social responsibility and he as a man — can only set a number of criteria, keeping which as the ultimate goal to achieve, the individual desirous of taking up the teaching profession should be selected.

One cannot set aside a very important aspect in teacher preparation work. This is the myriad and intricate type of human relationship that he finds himself involved in. His warmth of affection for so many pupils of all varying age and nature; considerate yet firm attitude towards their welfare and development — are unique elements that have a place only in teaching profession. This cannot be called mere attitude to the profession but a sophistication that goes with man, the superior being.

Selection Programme

Judged by the above standard, the current practices of selection and recruitment in the teachers' colleges are nowhere near the adequate standard.

(a) The admission to the B.Ed. programme in the two university departments of education is open to both men and women from all parts of the country as well as from countries abroad although local candidates are preferred. The minimum academic qualification for eligibility is a Bachelor's degree in Arts/Science/Commerce. But admission to the respective courses is subjected to qualifying in the B.Ed. admission tests. Candidates having Masters degree in Science/Arts in any division and a first graduation in science in second division are given preference in one university whereas, in the other it is insisted that the candidates must have offered at least two school subjects in the first degree examination. The admission tests generally, include, (i) an intelligence test, (ii) an English essay, (iii) a reading comprehension test and (iv) a test in any of the two school subjects. In the other university department, besides the general intelligence test, an essay and an oral tests are held. The personal interview of each candidate by the staff of the departments is obligatory and it is held that admission is strictly on merit in the combined performance in the admission tests and interview.

(b) The admission policy obtaining in the Regional Colleges of Education does not have to depend much on selection tests. It lays emphasis on a good academic record as well as an impressive interview.

Both the colleges are advantageously placed owing to their regional character and the stipendiary provisions (Rs. 75) for the students pursuing the courses of studies therein. However,the admission requirements for the one year B.Ed. course and the four-year Integrated courses are different. The one year B.Ed. programme requires a Bachelor degree in Science/Commerce/Agriculture on the part of the candidates seeking admission. Third divisioners are not debarred from making an application but due to the wide catchment area (in case of Bhopal — four States of Maharashtra, Goa, Gujarat and Madhya Pradesh) the one year B.Ed. students are essentially the second division degree holder or even better than that. Besides they are nominated by the State Governments of the adjoining States from amongst teachers who are in service but are untrained. Priority thus for admission is more or less in order of (i) teachers in multipurpose schools, (ii) teachers in non-multipurpose schools, and (iii) persons outside the teaching profession. One of the colleges specialises in training teachers, be it in one year course or 4 year course,in Science, Commerce, English and Agriculture, while the other one takes special care in subject area, *viz.*, Science, Home Science, Commerce, Agriculture and English. Third divisioners in higher secondary are generally not admitted to the 4-year course. Thus the two main criteria used for selecting candidates are, (a) past academic record, and (b) performance in the interview with a committee consisting of the College Principal, one or two senior members of the college faculty, sometimes the Head of the Department and the representative of the State Department of Education. The college, however, has the final say in the matter of selection of candidates.

(c) The admission policy can be of extreme measures also as in some training departments, the authorities do not believe in arranging for any admission tests or interview, in the 95% of the short listed candidates selected have to qualify themselves through the strict screening as arranged by the college authorities. In the sample case histories of institutions three colleges fall into this category.

Of the two types mentioned above, the former follows an arrangement where teachers are trained exclusively for one special branch, say, Home Science. Here a second class student in B.Sc. Home Science is eligible for the course and admitted also without having to go through any admission or selection test. In the latter category falls one college of Education where 80% of students admitted to the B.Ed. course are the untrained teachers in service in government schools. They are deputed straightaway to the Government maintained teachers' college. The admission policy governs the selection of the rest 20% of the candidates who have to compete on two aspects, namely, — (i) science, home science, geography, mathematics, music and drawing and painting fetch them a preference, and (ii) a personal interview with a panel of college teachers and the principal helps in the selection procedure. Generally, candidates with a first division in the Bachelor's degree get selected.

Perhaps one teachers' college selects 95% of its student trainees after devising quite a thorough procedure of selection. (i) The college arranges for one test in General Information and three objective type tests in 3 school subjects. (ii) Each of these tests and interview carry 5 marks. (iii) the division obtained by the candidate from Matriculation to M.A. is separately assigned 3, 2 and 1 credit each respectively for First, Second and Third division. (iv) To give preference to science graduates, a credit of 2 marks is assigned to B.Sc. candidates. (v) For record performance in extra-curricular activities during pre-training period a credit of 3 marks is allotted. (vi) Credits to the tune of 2 marks are kept for any publication of articles in any journal. (vii) Pre-training teaching experience is given credit of marks to the extent of 3 for 4 years, 4 for up to 6 years, 5 for up to 8 years and 6 for more than 8 years teaching experience. (viii) The head teacher of an elementary school or an Elementary Education Officer gets another credit of 5 marks. Now the candidates who obtain 50% of the total marks enumerated above are admitted. The college enjoys the privilege to select 10% of the candidate after 90% are selected in the elaborate way outlined above. But it has been the experience that 95% of the B.Ed. students are selected through normal procedure and only 5% of the candidates may fall into the teachers' quota.

(d) There are institutions which cannot have a uniform admission policy, however, much they realise its importance. Or rather admission policy works under local administration of government pressures from time to time. Two such institutions do not have any procedure of selection tests at all. One of them works by giving top priority to candidates with a degree/degrees in Science subjects in preference even to post-graduate qualifications in any Arts subjects. Hence the Department admits students only on the basis of past academic record. A privately managed institute as it is, it is amenable to pressures and influences to the extent of selecting about 20% of the candidates who are otherwise less meritorious.

As an institution affiliated to the university, another teachers' college is guided by an admission policy as prescribed by the university although it is eager to adopt a scientific basis of testing as a prelude to admission. The college decides to allot 4 points on the academic merit and 8 points for a personal interview by the college interview board. Candidates are finally selected on the basis of their combined performance (in the selection) at these two levels.

A rigorous selection procedure is prevalent in an institution which follows the similar pattern of teacher training but prefers candidates with M.A. in English and M.Scs. over all other subjects. If this is considered equivalent to academic merit, the candidate's performance on the written tests and interview receives considerable importance. The written tests include an essay in a language, a general knowledge test, an intelligence test and a reading and dictation test. Although it considers the testing pattern as satisfactory, the college records show that it is not fully free to act according to its selection procedure as administratively and financially it acts often under pressure of influencing agencies.

An analysis of the admission policy and practices thus reveal the extent of divergence that exists in the selection of students for teaching. Local variations exist, local pressure and demands too influence the selection. A certain amount of importance is assigned justifiably to the academic standing of the candidates because a teacher after all will have to have the mastery of knowledge over a field of specific study.

Summing up

The selection practices for teacher training, as examined here, reveal a wide variety of procedures ranging from a total absence of it to an elaborate testing procedure. In places where the teacher training course is concerned with a special subject area, two modes of admission are in vogue, (i) the applicants are directly recruited on the basis of their past academic record and the percentage of marks they have obtained in the university exams; (ii) the candidates who are the specialist teachers in different subject fields and are deputed by the State Government, for training. There is then no need for any admission test for them. The admission policy is governed by a special consideration.

Of the various techniques for the selection of teacher trainees used by the teacher training colleges, 'interviewing the applicants' is widely in vogue. It is held that experienced personnel already in the field, that is, the teacher educators, possess an ability to assess the qualities of the would-be-teachers in a brief and curt dialogue with the candidates. Such interviews definitely have a goal and that is to select or not to select a candidate for training, but such interviews should proceed along a well developed schedule prepared and kept ready by the college faculty. In such a situation the interviewers are likely to direct the interviewee to a climate wherein they can make more or less a proper estimate of the latter's ability to pursue the course than from a mere impression in a few minutes. There is the need to develop a 'somewhat' uniform set of criteria to make the task of interviewing objective.

Intelligence test figures as a second common technique used for trainee selection. The tests are of as wide variety as the notion of intelligence is. Are they the standardised tests? Have there been good studies to establish relationship between effective teaching and intelligence? The whole arrangement may help only in the matter of screening candidates.

Tests of general knowledge might be in keeping with teacher's scholarship. It is commonly believed that a widely read person has an aptitude for reading and acquiring wide knowledge. This will add to his academic distinction and professional confidence.

Tests in school subjects figured in some centres. True enough, that this testing is with a view to ascertaining the competence of the applicants in their respective fields of study. But haven't the universities acted as proper agencies to establish that part of the ability of the would-be-teachers? Do such tests measure other objectives besides pure information? And school teaching would require a varied range of academic objectives.

An attempt is made to test the language competence in some teachers' colleges by arranging to test the ability to comprehend and express in English or in mother tongue. Either of these languages is primarily used as the communication medium.

It seems the aptitude, interest and attitudes to teaching profession are by and large remaining outside the perview of testing. Under the prevailing indecisive state of affairs a systematic planning towards teacher selection, does not seem to be existing. Candidates recruited without any admission test for teacher training are treated at par in the job fields with those who struggle hard to obtain admission in some training colleges. Then how does one justify the rigorous admission practices in some colleges.

Langeveld's comment on this problem is very apt when he says, "sufficiently precise criteria for their selection do not exist and the process, therefore, does not at present deserve the name of selection."[1] However, when a person considers his choice of career and thinks about the teaching profession, he must be led to consider the different functions of the teacher. The experiment in Sweden during the forties and fifties of the present era on how well were the impact of educational reforms accepted by the teachers in service and the intending teachers recorded significant results. It is seen that intending teachers who were better informed, about the school reform were more inclined towards such changes and adaptation that followed. A positive attitude and an increased information during teacher training helped in effective implementation of important measures. Hence orientation to the nature of the job and the job fitness are the pre-requisites of the training programme as well as the selection procedure and the latter ought to be made more scientific and functional.

1. M.J. Langeveld. The *Psychology of Teachers and the Teaching Profession*. The Year Book of Education. 1963 Evans Brothers Limited, London.

5

Curriculum in Teacher Education

What is a teacher expected to do when he is in service? He has to teach several groups of students in a school and he teaches either one subject or more than one as the situation in the school, where he is placed, demands. He stays in the school for at least five to six hours. Besides his classroom teaching he may have to be in charge of several out-of-class activities, say, co-curricular items for the growth and development of the children under his charge. Further he has to understand and discharge the various organisational and administrative duties of the school as and when required, *viz.*, frame time table, decide the implementation of course work set for the different class groups, conduct examination and prepare progress reports, arrange school functions, maintain records, attend and organise meetings and so on. He is also expected to maintain a pleasant human relation with all concerned.

For the execution of varied type of jobs of which a few only are mentioned above, a teacher needs a thorough orientation in a number of experiences. First he acts as a (i) director of learning, second as a (ii) motivator and guide to students and third as (iii) maintainer and executor of order and discipline in the running of the school. However, there is a big gap between what he does and what is expected of him.

Teacher: Director of Learning

As a director of learning a teacher has to be a fully educated person to be able to function effectively and fully in his every-day classroom situations. He has to maintain perpetually a contact with his field of study as best as he can, enlarge the horizon of his learning in order to give the benefit of the same to the young learners. Acquiring knowledge in a field is best cultivated when the knowledge is communicated to the batch of learners. This calls for professional competence which comprises planning of lessons, possessing requisite knowledge of the subject matter, perceiving how pupils learn, executing the proposed plan of activity, encouraging the learner to help himself and testing how much he has learnt. Curiously enough the teacher architect sees his edifice installed in the learner's growth. The teaching-learning process moves from a so-called tangible plan of activity to the most intangible plan where sky is the only limit for any attainment. A true director of learning should be an expert reconnaitre of the field of learning wherein, in one sweep he assesses his own ability as well as the efforts of his learners. Therefore, he must (a) know his own depth of learning, (b) have desire, aptitude and ability to communicate, (c) possess a limitless patience and zeal and (d) act to help transform individuals into a better and happier living models. Removing all pretentions one admits that a beginning teacher begins by depending heavily on arrangement of the course content at the outset. He is just an apprentice and as such he has yet not gained in confidence, far less he can be expected to handle the intricacies of human learning efficiently. It is the years' experience in teaching that will establish him on a surer and firmer footing in his job. When he begins to teach he is more often concerned about the subject matter than anything else. Over the years he gains greater facility in the knowledge content and he devotes more time to student learning. It is a voyage, so to say, from subject centeredness to learner centeredness. He develops concern about his pupils' all-round welfare gradually. One does not become a 'director' of learning without putting in years of labour to the making of it.

Teacher: Motivator and Guide

To be able to motivate one requires a good deal of self motivation. It is assumed that his own intelligent participation in the planning and implementation of school's curricular and co-curricular programme inspires the learners' group. The very nature of activities would speak of him as an agent of change and progress. His creative zeal and imagination ignites similar spark in the younger group and opens before them a direction for further improvement and personal-social fulfilment. A teacher has to recognise the potential talents of all varieties. Richer his socio-cultural background better is his playing the role of the director. His dynamism counts in developing leadership qualities. He is supposed to transcend the existing boundaries of culture and values and install, if possible, a better tomorrow. Teacher's own personality, his knowledge about his learners' environment, their growth potential and his ability to be forward-looking are matters for consideration in this particular dimension.

Teacher: Organiser

A teacher has to execute a good amount of organisational and administrative duties in his professional life. This requires a high degree of sense of responsibility, a knowledge of code of conduct and service rules and their bearing on day to day managerial activities. He has to have an ability to maintain certain amount of dignity, poise and self-respect to face all rough and smooth weather. This attribute in a teacher definitely grows with years of experience and no amount of make-believe situations in a training college will offer a learning experience to the student teacher in this aspect. The above analysis should be kept in mind while examining the curriculum of a teacher training college. It is necessary to establish if there is a close matching between the work schedule of the teacher in a school and the programme adopted for teacher preparation in a training college.

Objectives of Teacher Training

The Training College in India aims broadly:

(a) to develop some basic insight into and understanding of some concepts, principles of education in general and with reference to education in vogue in a particular country;
(b) to develop an understanding of human nature, the growth and development of human individual right through various stages;
(c) to develop knowledge and insight as how an individual learns and makes use of his environment in the process of growing;
(d) to develop an awareness of his capacity to teach after duly analysing the skills, aptitudes and ability which compose such capacity;
(e) to initiate the student teachers to practise the skill of teaching, *viz.*, to plan a lesson, to face groups of students from time to time, to deliver lessons effectively, to know his own ability to do the job and so on;
(f) to initiate the student teacher to understand the psychology of learners and the psychology of learning, to understand and practise some techniques of assessing and recording students' achievements;
(g) to consider participation of students in co-curricular activities essential to the growth of social skills, recreational temper and a balanced personality; and
(h) to consider learning as a never-ending process and to accept it as a valuable occupation as long as the teacher continues to remain in his job of teaching.

Are the Aims Realized

Though it is necessary that the student teachers should be helped to develop healthy attitude, broad based interest and values consistent with the dignity of the teaching profession and thereafter, develop a personality too, it is not possible for a training college during the short duration of the course and the limited resources in hand to achieve these ends. To some extent the existing training programme may possibly lay emphasis in giving shape to the 'director of learning' in the sense that two-thirds of the courses aim at doing that and that only. It is so because the running of such programme follows a more tangible and concrete plan, the success of which is easy to assess and establish. Besides, such course rests on the academic background which a student teacher has acquired prior to his professional training course. In the atmosphere of the training college, right from the practice of teaching skill to the activities motivating personal and professional growth much artificiality prevails. Hardly any effect is carried over to the schools by the students when they join schools as a teacher. Further, the sense of belongingness to a profession and the awareness of fuller responsibility of a regular teacher in a school, cannot be expected to grow in a new teacher. These two qualities can develop on a continued interaction between the teacher and his working organisation. Experience in the training college shows that no opportunity comes handy which can inculcate such mature understanding during their stay in the training college. Therefore, something that a teacher does in a school, does not get a place in a training college and equally valid is the statement that something that training college has got within its curriculum has little bearing on the school practice.

Whenever the teacher educators have assembled to suggest changes in the curriculum of teachers, colleges, it appears that suggestions evolve around the same classification of theory and practice papers. Or, at the most, attempts are made to spell out broad objectives of teacher education programme of the country. It may be (i) to specify the objectives of school programme, (ii) to do a job analysis of a teacher's task, (iii) to consider the feasibility of designing a plan for the teacher training for a duration of nine months and (iv) to determine weightage and priority of various aspects of the curriculum. This arrangement may put a stop to all criticisms that training college programmes are best forgotten the moment a trainee steps out of such an institution. This has also given rise to what is sometimes disparagingly known as 'the training college method' and the 'school method'. And in the actual field of work a new teacher in a school is briefed unhesitatingly by senior members that the former will do better if he pushes aside the learning of the training college.

Organising Teacher Education Programme

Then how best to organise the teacher education programme?

We want a teacher to be a knowledgeable person, who is well qualified, besides having a taste for reading and acquiring information all round. So it is essential that he maintains a living contact with the academic discipline. For that matter the various university departments or some representative centres must be the perennial source of guidance for him. Unfortunately, the teacher educators, by and large, over the years lose contact with the new developments in the university departments as they concentrate more on school curricula. This gap is seldom bridged because the method masters develop more clarity, depth and thereby greater expertise in guiding the ways and means of handling each topic in the school syllabus. It is admitted that only with the changes in the school curriculum, which is not very much the function of the university, a new challenge is felt by the training college staff. Otherwise, changes in the university curriculum do not get normally reflected in the school studies after years of waiting. Hence the task of preparation of teachers for schools suffer from a number of limitations, (i) growth of content knowledge stagnates, (ii) methodology, oft repeated, gets stale and the routine work gets into a rut, (iii) contact with academic disciplines becomes weak. For example, a teacher educator who specialises in English is engaged to prepare teachers of English for schools. His contact with university department of English is less maintained as he concentrates more on handling the English syllabus for the schools. One who teaches educational psychology in the B.Ed. programmes does have very little contact with the university department of psychology. This drawback impoverishes the teacher educator, although he develops excellent insight and skill in giving guidance for school teaching.

Principles of Education

A student teacher should know the fundamental of education in respect of sociopolitical and economic background. The meaning of education, the objectives, the socio-cultural and politico-economic background, various agencies that influence education, the principles that guide construction of curriculum are a few items among the thematic content. He has to analyse problems spread over extremes such as sex education to religious education. Some educational experiments, here and abroad and a knowledge about the activities of the educators are both expected to inspire him to make fresh and new ventures in education. This orientation is deemed necessary for a teacher in the making to enable him to learn to acquire information, to analyse issues and problems to communicate views and ideas, to arrive at judgment, to acquire proper power of expression, in short to feel free to hold views and freer still to argue for or against an issue. The whole experience connected with the details mentioned above seems to be the content of a very major theory paper. These topics do not have any direct relevance to the job of a teacher in a school. Still a teacher studies the course content of the theory. An awareness of the problems pertaining to living which the above outline aims to develop, is necessary for any adult member. Since this has not been developed in the student teachers before at any stage of living, its inclusion in the course is justified. But the learning experiences are far less commendable. Within short duration of 9 months, a proper preparation towards a good orientation seems impossible. Hence they are treated as topics to be covered very much through lectures. The purpose of making teacher education somewhat broadbased gets defeated. The benefits for such learning is never long enduring. The overall enrichment programme remains on the outskirts of the learner's experience, because making inroads to the learner's existence is a time consuming task. There is no guarantee that the most democratic personality in the training college turns out to be democratic in the long run. In a hurry, the student teacher covers the topics 'by points rather than lives' through the experiences. To claim that situations are created in a number of ways (mainly through co-curricular experiences) is to belittle the importance of experiences. The training college, cannot provide, except for a few good students, chances to all trainees to gain a worthwhile programme or experience. Therefore, the areas that need improvement are, (i) allowing more time to learners to do good reading for a sound build up of the intellect and attitude, (ii) pruning the existing course, (iii) arranging for experiences of exchanges other than merely attending lectures, and (iv) changing completely the mode of testing the inputs. Infact, the whole course need to be looked into from the angle of its need and relevance to life and activities in a school. If the life in a school could be taken as a base, the democratic living and the steps necessary to prepare for such living would give all relevance and significance to some such discussions in the teacher education programme.

Educational Psychology

Knowing the child in all his stages or development and in the numerous aspects of his growth assumes a big mass of information necessary for the teachers to master. This is for facilitating overall guidance — educational, personal, social, intellectual and the like — to the child at school. It is believed that such knowledge of psychology develops the knowledge of self concept in a teacher and adds to his mental well-being, because he learns to be conscious of his own self in the process. The conditions in the school are such that such valuable experience gained in the training college do not find a justifiable use in the school. While it is recognised that the matter is useful if there is a scope to find its application, it is also admitted that within the rigid programme of the school, the very implications are forgotten. The book learning fades away as time advances. Still, it is one of the most important and heavy theory courses in the B.Ed. programme. The concept of the school as a miniature society may bring in the interplay of psychology and sociology. The liveable experience must then begin the 'practice way'. The psychological bearing should start from the sociological angle where the typical Indian outlook is focussed in building up the thesis of 'understanding the learner', and not the other way round. Thus, educational psychology for Indian schools has to have an exclusive trademark of Indian society.

There are two ways of looking at the teacher education programme, *viz.*, (i) looking at the curriculum from the angle of the school and (ii) looking at it from the angle of the training college. In India, Schools or School Boards of Education have hardly any say in the matter of planning the teacher preparation course. But it is this body that stand at one end playing the role of biggest consumers of the turn-outs of training colleges. Had they had a say in the matter or had there been an easy interchangeability of the school staff and training college staff, much of the objections with regard to non-applicability of training college experiences in the school situations would not have existed.

The situation obtaining at present, however, is different. Training colleges having conceived of or imagined a certain perspective in the functioning and behaviour of a teacher in a school, chalked out (ever since 1937) a programme of action. It may be that this programme or the curriculum is followed more to the interest and benefit of the training colleges than the school because quite a few experiences provided for in the teacher's college do not find proper appreciation in the school. Similarly, in the day to day execution of school duties, several situations arise, which are completely missing in the teacher education programme. For example, completing a year's syllabus for a particular grade within a limited time length, in the best possible way so as to result in the best achievements in the class is a herculean task. This is what the training college is harping at. But how seldom such an experience is made available to the student teacher. Handling of different audiovisual aids or making such aids on the spot for just 50% of the classes in a day's teaching schedule is a rare sight in a school. But the teacher educator is always emphasising its importance. Democratic handling of the class group, teacher-student planning in completing courses, planning and executing co-curricular activities and alongside emphasising its vital importance in the growth of personality of the school children — all these seem to constitute the utopian scheme outside the school. Examples can be multiplied. So there is less corroboration between the need of the two organisations — the school and the training college. No wonder that the B.Ed. Revision Programme, undertaken by the Department of Teacher Education, NCERT, as late as 1969, March fails to throw any new light in the B.Ed. curriculum revision. The work envisaged the good old task of (1) spelling out teacher education objectives, (2) dividing the course work into four broad areas, namely, educational psychology and other optional papers in the same field, (3) problems and history of Indian education, (4) practical part of the B.Ed. programme, and (5) leading the three groups of participants to work out the details of each head mentioned above. The syllabus that has been proposed is a revision or rearrangement of the existing curriculum and not a fresh planning under the demands of the new social pattern and outlook in the country.

Another consideration comes for close scrutiny. Our rural and urban set ups are so distinctly different from one another. Our training colleges are aware of this big gap but proper orientation to the need of the environment appears some-what absent in the programme of the teacher education centres. Those teachers who are posted in the rural schools, if their training had been completed in the urban centres, find themselves semimisfits with a patch up make up between rural background and urban modernism. This situation highlights another serious need in the country's teacher education programme. There has not been any significant breakthrough in our attempt to plan out teacher education programme suitable to only rural needs and rural environment.

From the training college side two types of curriculum are in vogue, *viz.*, (a) curriculum for one year B.Ed. course and (b) an integrated four-year course. One-year post-graduation B.Ed. course is the more common programme of teacher education throughout the country. Sometimes these institutions prepare teachers for all school subjects. At other places, *i.e.*, Regional Colleges, the one-year courses are offered in specific subjects, such as, Home Science, Fine Arts, Commerce, Agriculture, Science and Technology to university graduates. The four integrated courses pursued in Regional colleges are offered in Science, Technology and English to those who have passed the Pre University course or Higher Secondary Examination. The basic policy underlying such a course is that, the education of a teacher, based broadly on a foundation of general education should include a thorough mastery of subject matter so as to give him an insight into its structure and interrelationships and professional preparation. The aim is to bring about an integration of general education, specialization, and professional course content. Evidently the curriculum with regard to (i) Theory and (ii) Practice in the two courses 1-year and 4-year are different. Which of the two syllabi offer a better deal is yet to see.

The New Trend

With the introduction of the new pattern of school education (10+2) more significant changes in the teacher education course will be necessary.

In 1975, NCERT has proposed a new Secondary Teacher Education Curriculum in view of the 10+2 pattern. The objectives are few but well contained. The Committee have retained the objectives as suggested in the Conference on Revision of B.Ed. programme, held in Calcutta, March 23 to 26, 1969. These objectives are spelt out into specific ones classified under understanding, skills and attitudes. The programme as chalked out consists of 1000 marks — Theory Paper — 600 marks and Practical Work — 400 marks, of which 250 marks are for Practice-in-Teaching.

The outline in each Paper appears to include some new features. For example, in Paper called Philosophical and Sociological Foundation of Education, topics like Social determinants of educational attainments in India and 'School as a social institution for organised instruction' are very appropriate. The part of 'School Organisation' is very aptly appended to this very Paper. The orientation to their field of work is likely to be of promise. For the first time practical work for every Paper has been suggested. The burden of the discipline of Psychology is reduced considerably but made more meaningful. The course entitled Problems of Indian Education in Historical Perspectives starts since 1937 and does justice to modern trends and current problems in the country.

A departure from any previous curriculum is 'Optional Special Field Papers.' It is a changed list no doubt. There is a provision to offer 'Advanced Methodology in teaching one of the School subjects.' This Paper should normally be allowed to good Honours or Master degree holders, and it should prepare them, *inter-alia* for training college work in that subject. Their practice teaching will also be weighted towards this subject *i.e.*, such candidates may do about 2/3rd of practice teaching in this area and must handle at least two stages in the school. This course may be taken by teachers who will be taking classes 11th and 12th as suggested in the new scheme.

The next aspect in the new curriculum is the 'Minimum Essential Practical Work' which fall into two sections, (i) Class Room Teaching and (ii) Other Work comprising, (a) Social Community Work, (b) Practical work connected with Theory Papers and (c) Development of Social attitudes and personality traits.

It is heartening to note the new Curriculum Committee put strong stress on the need for experimentation and innovation in the curriculum for teacher preparation work. "It can be said that hardly any attempt seem to have been made to frame a curriculum on the basis of any sound scientific evidence in regard to the different parts of units of the curriculum recommended for adoption. Even the one recommended by the Calcutta group of teacher educators is based upon their opinions and not on any scientific or experimental or objective criteria. However, the programme marks an advancement in suggesting a more functional curriculum for the preparation of secondary school teachers for tommorrow."[1]

In this seventh decade of the twentieth century very brisk activities in organising Secondary Teacher Education Curriculum are going on in the four corners of the country. As National Bodies on Education, both UGC and National Council of Teacher Education, NCERT have arranged several National Conferences — in May, 1976 at Simla, in November, 1976, in Madras, and in February, 1977, in New Delhi and also in March, 1977 in New Delhi to reconstruct teacher education programme with a view to improving the quality of the teacher. Although a tentative programme, the latest one as has been chalked out by the National Council of Teacher Education NCERT, in their 'Teacher Education Curriculum' (A Framework) aptly emphasises 3 broad areas, namely,

(a)	Pedagogical Theory	(weightage 20%)
(b)	Working with the Community	(weightage 20%)
(c)	Content-*cum*-Methodology and Practice Teaching, including Related Practical work.	(weightage 60%)

1. Secondary Teacher Education Curriculum — NCERT, 1975.

The area (a) is supposed to comprise Education in Indian Sociological Perspectives, Functional use of features of Educational Psychology and some special courses related to the needs and conditions of the area or region where the teacher preparation task will be undertaken.

Area (b) specifies "Working with the Community". It is a novel and at the same time a useful venture, more so in the changed context of the Indian Society today. It has suggested a few activities that can be localised in rural areas. Variation of the rural and urban areas, in less developed and more developed areas will require numerous such projects. Flexibility of approach in the selection and implementation of such activity is the keynote behind such suggestions.

In Area (c) around the classroom needs, specific learning experiences have been planned. For example, a teacher must know certain general principles and techniques to use in the classroom; he should be able to teach at least two subjects of his choice — the subject grouping could be one of the five — (i) Life Sciences, (ii) Physical Sciences, (iii) Social Sciences, (iv) Languages and (v) Mathematics. Again the field of work experience offers him an opportunity to learn one of the many work; his role as a guide in respect of health preservation and health hazards cannot be forgotten. Furthermore, for all his efficiency in teaching he has to master certain skills.

The proposed restructuring of the teacher education programme has certainly become an exercise in bringing into such a plan a functional and realistic approach. The emphasis has been to strike a compromise between a more practical and service oriented and a less theoretically heavy course for the future teachers. This itself is commendable. Still, it may take us a decade more to shed off the love for intellectual platitudes that often with best of intentions is not fully sacrificed in developing any realistic programme in our country. The needs of the community *vis-a-vis* the need and efficiency of the teacher are awaiting a concrete and first-hand exploration. On the foundation of such surveys and direct contact can the teacher education programme be planned properly. The planners know how to take off from the conventional route but they are not yet ready for a voyage or a plunge into a fresh horizon. Perhaps by breaking through new grounds we will be able to vitalise the rural sector, and this is undoubtedly the need of the hour.

6

Student Teaching in Teacher Education Programme

The art of teaching started with teaching itself. Much before the theory papers were thought about and much before any general preparedness was sounded, a teacher began doing his work by beginning to teach. For the development of his competencies in teaching, his practical experiences gave him a kind of 'feedback' every now and then. He learnt to modify his method or technique of teaching a particular unit at a time when his own technique did not work. Or, greater still was the compelling need of the pupils. Doubtless then, practice-in-teaching is the central theme constituting the key experiences in the teacher education programme.

The 'ding-dong' battle between technique and content in the training of teachers will not serve any purpose in the modern era. Then how important is the question of acquiring mastery in the technique of teaching. In the opinion of Edmund King, "Technique does not educate or humanise; it merely provides the wherewithal for human consumption. . . . is thought to be a dehumanising brute necessity for some. True culture is remote from this." According to him, one should much rather be aware of a sense of social responsibility which alerts one to a changing life. And viewed from the angle, a teacher is less of an 'external practitioner' and more of a partner in the task of social change. Continuing with some argument the alleged improvement of a teacher's education should not consist of mere subject enlargement or social climbing or pre-occupation with tricks of techniques.

Still in our economically less developed country, simple literacy will remain one of the major objectives of our school systems. Moreover, successfully harnessing of our educational system to industrial and commercial development of the country will be emphasised for several decades to come. This should explain perhaps that, however, dehumanising effect 'techniques' can have for some considerable number of years, the 'ideal' teacher in our soil may have to be understood as one who has to carry the sceptre of traditional dichotomy of 'liberal education' and 'vocational training'.

In our country the role of a teacher has been for long to transmit the body of information and knowledge to the classroom. This helps in the realisation of an immediate goal and that is enabling pupils to pass the examination. This is an extremely limited goal and the existing training programme offers a kind of practice teaching experience which prepares only a fractional teacher, a teacher who is a classroom technician in the task of dispensing of knowledge. He takes upon himself the task of initiating and completing all teaching learning activities and soon acquires an attitude of complacency in this one-way communication. Innovations are hardly seen, challenges are seldom provided, a docile set of pupils are turned out where conformity to controlled situations set as an ideal goal.

The situation in 'teaching' which assumes the focus of attention needs a little analysis. That a student teacher is required to complete a specified number of hours of teaching is undeniably accepted in all teacher preparation programme. In addition to several hours of classroom teaching, he has to undertake some practical work the impact of which is assumed to help make him a better and more skilful teacher. So within classroom and outside classroom experiences should be so arranged that they aim at identifying and developing the predominant Pedagogical abilities. When does a teacher become skilful? Pedagogic abilities are indicative of a potentiality that may enable a teacher to become skilful through the process of practice. Hence, teacher educators would do well to analyse these abilities, for the development of which both the teaching practice and other practical works are organised. The activities in themselves will prove futile if the pedagogical abilities cannot be developed in and through them.

Pedagogical Abilities for a Pupil Teacher

Pedagogical abilities are a set of properties which an individual must possess in order to show good results in teaching. These abilities have been enumerated as power of observation, imagination, tactfulness, a high sense of duty applicable to himself and others, organising ability and distributive attention. Working with these abilities is to sharpen the potentiality to achieve mastership.

The pedagogical power of observation should enable a teacher to see the tendencies of the development and formation of pupil's knowledge, skills and habits as well as the manifestation of the pupil's individuality. It is a capacity to penetrate into the students' mind, to estimate the main deficiencies in his knowledge, morals, etc., to notice the strongest points of his personality, nature, aptitudes, and habits, to make the best use of them for educational purposes. He has also to find out the pupil's affections and attachments for individuals and ideal things and motives in order to use their influences for the pupil education. Teaching practice should take care of all these.

In his ability of the pedagogical imagination, the teacher keeps a plan of direction for himself and progress for his pupil. He wishes to shape his pupil by helping to form the latter's habits, and behaviour on one hand and future activity with a wide range of interests on the other. His insight into the pupil's nature helps him to arrange the Educational work in such a way as to keep in mind the final purpose, promote the positive features of the pupil's personality, thus planning for the most remote future of the pupils. Deep in his imagination then is the desire and capacity to mould educational measures from time to time and to improve the educational process.

A sense of duty to oneself always motivates the group of learners so much so that pupils readily learn to submit to the teachers' educational influence. It is at best a habit which the teacher has used for himself and it acts as a kind of 'prop' for the pupils in their growth and seriousness of purpose. His strictness which he applies to himself, fetches him due sense of respect and sense of discipline in habit and work from the students.

What is pedagogical tactfulness? It is the ability to establish the correct relations with the pupils, intelligent communication with colleagues to maintain a sense of proportion in mutual demands and satisfaction. This quality of character is likely to save many delicate psychological problems that may arise in all educational endeavour, be it with colleagues or pupils, parents or administrators.

Distributive attention is a great virtue in a teacher. It is with this ability that he keeps all children together and every child separately. This unique knack in a teacher endear him to the pupil group because the individual child wants to be appreciated and respected by the love and attention of the grown-ups.

The teacher cannot miss the importance of organising ability. Right from organising his lesson he is required to arrange for all kinds of social and recreational and vocational activities. The power of organisation will deepen the sense of purpose, fruitful gain, an avoidance of waste of all kinds. The influence of such an ability is great on the pupils' environment. Take for instance our country. In a country like ours, rich and colourful as the community behaviour is, the teacher acts as a great influence in helping to perpetuate the glamour and grandeur of traditions through his pupils. Educational institutions attach a lot of importance to cultural activities and the traditional significance that goes with each such item. To work towards a fine display of cultural performance, the pupils need to have a thorough background information of the particular activity, an attitude to gain from an exchange of ideas and feelings, a mood and temper to participate and practice in all activities of broader social and cultural dimensions and to learn to develop aesthetic and artistic taste.

The question of participation calls for the sensitivity and a broad awareness of social needs as well as a sense of personal responsibility — a very difficult area indeed to touch upon. Culture of a land is sustained provided it is rooted upon the cultivation of worthy habits and sentiments as much as avoidance of conflicting gestures and conservative ideas.

A teacher has also to work under lot of constraint, specially in a developing country with long heritage. Economic difficulties in terms of restricted grants of funds and more stringent measures to choose priorities to chanallise those funds and to avoid wastage of all kinds, loom large heavily with the dispenser of knowledge, the teacher. This is far more serious a consideration in the preparation of teachers and their pedagogical arts and ability than in pure and simple training of teachers in an economically solvent land. It is often seen that the meaning behind a learning concept does not so much depend on accumulation of facts as it does on first hand experience made available to the learner. The teacher's pedagogical abilities are never to be seen as alienated from pupil's involvement, pleasure and profit.

The pedagogical abilities of a teacher are not all confined to teacher's needs. These are sometimes combined with some special aptitudes. He has a special command over some branches of knowledge, he has talents and interests in non-academic fields as well which makes his personal and professional life rather complete and satisfying. Such a combination of abilities leads to high educational achievements.

Development of Pedagogical Abilities

There is no conclusive proof that the formation of these abilities is a direct result of the subjects the pupil teacher has studied. But equally undisputed is the fact that the childhood years of a human being are the most favourable period for the development of these tendencies. Observing the school teacher's ability and performance, helping classmates and others with their tasks, participating actively in the social life of the school help develop the power of observation and imagination. Organising ability, sense of duty and sympathy — began to develop in an individual. Such personalities in the teaching profession are an asset. The teacher educator finds his task of educating the pupil teacher 'smooth running' and enjoyable when trainees are those who have already acquired scientific knowledge of matter of study and an understanding of educational problems.

The Value of School Practice

Teaching abilities are formed during school practice. The trainee is responsible for teaching his special subject or subjects, for introducing new material in accordance with the syllabus. It takes time for him to decide the pace at which the class can best work. He acts as an assistant to the regular teacher in the practice teaching school and he looks up to the latter for all kinds of assurances and inspiration. If he is helped to solve concrete pedagogical problems by his senior colleague in the school he gains tremendously in understanding the application of what is learned in the training college. This is the period when he learns to 're-vision' the field of knowledge on one hand and to develop the art of putting it across to the class in a meaningful way. He learns to control and direct the children's behaviour as much as his own psychological activity. The more responsible and well-informed he is, the more difficulties he feels in preparing his lessons, the better are the lessons he gives. In the process of practice teaching he acquires the powers of observation, attention, teaching imagination and a sense of time. He learns how to prepare his lessons independently and how to mark pupil's work.

During school practice, the trainee arrives at some independent conclusions which are likely to form his pedagogic convictions. He improves upon his deficiencies. The individuality of the young teacher is perceived when he works independently at school. He should be given a chance to show his own initiative and creative work. He should be critically evaluating his own teaching capacities.

All teachers do not master their profession at once. The decisive moment in the life of a young teacher is when he faces serious difficulties which stimulate his desire to overcome them. He becomes conscious of his vocation. Certain change then takes place — it may be sudden or slow, it may happen either during school practice or at a little later stage when he is in service.

Requirements for teacher education, in our set up rightfully put emphasis on practice-in-teaching and some sessional practical work. Just the enumeration of the 'Practical Work' is a list — rich and varied — ranging from school assignments, projects, to psychology practicals and visual education. Besides it constitutes craft work, community services and co-curricular activities. The programme of practical work is intended to strengthen the school practice of the student teacher when he is under training and later to add to the dimension of his role as a teacher in service. But in the planning and implementation of such practical work, it makes a very poor show. Usually these activities assume importance so long as the pupil are under training. The activities are evaluated separately by numerical marking and they are independent of practice teaching marks. Very little of the impact of such activities are carried over to the school practice field. The marks are kept separate from each other and there has not been studies conducted to show that trainees who score high in practical school work, do necessarily score high in teaching practice or *vice versa*. The pedagogical abilities are thus seldom analysed for our trainees; nor are the practical activities planned and carried through with a view to sharpening the pedagogical abilities. It seems practice teaching stands on one end of the scale of practical experience having little to do with the practical work. How do the activities, as outlined, have come to be clubbed together need some probe. Their bearing on the quality of teaching needs thorough research. One can perhaps call these two parts as complementary.

The observations can be made here. (i) The teaching practice abilities are different in nature. The benefits of practical work which are in the training college programme do not very much relate themselves to the reinforcement of the skills in practice teaching. (ii) If school practice skills have got to be sharpened, the training college should plan a fresh type of practical work than those in vogue.

The practice teaching programme deserves an independent treatment now. Some data can be presented below.

In a study (R.C. Srivastava,[1] Chapter II) involving 82 teacher training institutions, nearly ten followed the Diploma course in teaching and the rest the Degree course. Of the institutions offering degree courses in education, little above 74 percent of the colleges require a trainee to undergo instruction only in the theory aspect of the professional education and to do some practical work in the nature of practice-in-teaching and some sessional work deemed to be connected with practice teaching. In the rest 25% of the institutions of the same category some insist on even instructions and examination in items of craft work, community service and language and subject content. The ten institutions that

1. R.C. Srivastava: Evaluation of Practice Teaching in Teacher-Training Institutes, Delhi-7. C.I.E. Studies, 1970.

followed the Diploma course prescribed compulsory community service or craft-*cum*-community service and the like. Thus it seems that practical work is very much a compulsory item in the teacher education programme and that it is meant to strengthen the practice-in-teaching experience.

Secondly, the weightage given to the practice teaching differs from institution to institution. Marks assigned to the practical work which include practice teaching and sessional practical work range from a little less than 30% to as high as 100% of the theory marks. Moreover, the trend is to give relatively less weightage to the practical work. Three universities give equal weightage in terms of marks to theory and practical work.

Thirdly, the distribution of marks over practice teaching, sessional practical work again shows differences in different institutions. Marks are found equally distributed between practice teaching and practical sessional work in about 33% of the institutions: in near about 20% institutions the trainees are assessed only in practice teaching; in 47% of institutes, practice teaching has larger weightage than sessional work and in one institution (Jamia Millia Islamia) practical teaching gets 25% of marks whereas 75% of marks are kept for sessional work. It is strangely evident that opinions differ as regards the degree of importance to be assigned to the two major divisions namely, the school teaching and the practical work in the teacher education programme.

Fourthly, to obtain a pass in the practical aspect of the course the marks required range between 33% to 50% except in places where 'grades' are used. In some universities the first, second and third division of the awards in practical differ with regard to the magnitude of the marks. The distinction mark ranges from 65% to 70% percent, first division from 60% to 80% and the second ranging between 48% to 55% in different universities.

The data reveals another interesting finding. In some institutions the trainee does not have to pass the theory and practical examination separately. In some others, the university awards distinction on the aggregate of marks obtained in theory and practical work taken together. A different pattern obtains also where theory and practical results are declared separately. Again there are some institutions where a trainee who is not good enough in class teaching is even able to pass because of his better performance in practical sessional work.

A relative weightage in terms of marks indicate the significant position of practice teaching in a programme of professional education. Equally important criterion is the amount of time or hours of work a trainee has to complete in order to qualify for the degree. At least two school subjects a trainee has to offer and the number of total lessons to be delivered by a trainee varies from 25 to 80. In two Regional Colleges of Education the arrangement is for eight weeks internship and in Kurukshetra University, block teaching of six weeks' duration.

It seems that the place of student teaching is judged on several counts namely, its balance against theory, weightage in terms of marks, number of subjects to specialise in and number of lessons delivered and arrangement of practice teaching during the year of training and provisions for expert guidance and supervision when the candidate is under training.

Even after all kinds of elaborate arrangements regarding placing of practice-in-teaching are made, non-seriousness to the task of teaching, deficient sense of duty, irresponsibility, aim-lessness and indifference to children, lack of innovative measures in teaching are great obstacles to the development of pedagogical skill. There exists a certain amount of despondency when it is expressed that what is taught in a training college is neither worth practising nor is actually practised in schools. This section of the people believe, that some small skills and habits like planning of lessons, skill in questioning, use of black board do persist in the trained individual for a little while, but it fades away with years of teaching experience.

Finally, in the life of every good teacher there are periods when the whole orientation of their work gets revived and improved. Such developments of pedagogical abilities in his life may occur all of a sudden or at steady intervals. In the light of such experiences his pedagogical knowledge and skill widen. And that works as a sure impetus to a renewal of effort. But in how many cases of our trained teachers do we find such distinguished workers?

7

Organization of Student Teaching

With a view to developing an awareness of and a taste for professional preparation, 'practice-in-teaching' has been receiving a prime importance in the teacher training colleges. The teacher training institutes reserve a distinctive merit and a stamp of uniqueness in the organisation of practice teaching programme. This core programme in teacher education is woven around a number of practices that each student trainee must undergo in actual teaching situation. The number of lessons delivered by the trainees may vary from 40 to 90; nevertheless, the experience to be obtained through class teaching and the related activities are expected to provide a built-in structure for a future teacher. Although Classroom teaching for a number of periods assume the main importance, there are numerous small jobs that go with class teaching, which are given equal emphasis. The institutes then have to work hard in organising the comprehensive programme of student teaching.

GROUP ONE

Preparation for Student-Teaching

Looking at the current practices in the two university departments of education, it is noticed that the total number of lessons to be taught in two methods subjects show a wide range (90 in one and 40 in the other), but the arrangement of such a programme is handled with great care. The departments initiate the student teachers quite early into the teaching but not before they have gone through a 'pre-teaching' programme, normally of six weeks. During this period conscious efforts are made, so that, the faculty continues working on the development of ideas and practices regarding 'teaching' through their lectures, discussions and study guidance. Students are required to attend a course of lectures in the methods of teaching school subjects and also on other foundation papers. Discussions on lesson planning, on techniques of observation of a lesson conducted either by the method masters or a regular teacher in an attached experimental school, are held. It depends on the expertise and intention of the method masters as how they can make this experience a really rich and fruitful one. The lesson planning itself is a big task with all the various elements highlighted from time to time. Exhaustive discussions are held sometimes, on right from stating the objectives to evaluation of a lesson. Proper attention to the preparation of audio-visual aids is also paid. Proper use of the library is ensued.

Part-time Practice Teaching

It normally needs a month and a half since they join the course to put the trainees into actual classroom teaching situation. During this first phase of practice-in-teaching, the university department either send their pupils to several demonstration schools attached to the department or else to the same schools where the pupil teachers are to have their first teaching experience. For two weeks or so a trainee takes a class a day, discuss the lesson after executing the teaching plan. The theory classes continue to be held simultaneously in the college. This is the period when students are made to teach at least five of the lessons, the plans of which have been discussed and guidance from the method specialists on the faculty received. Near about 15 to 20 lessons in two subjects are completed during this first phase of practice teaching.

Block Teaching

The second phase of actual teaching practice is normally conducted in a block. A degree of mature experience can be expected from them by January and February, that is the last phase of their practice teaching. College classes on theory of education are kept suspended and student experiences a full-time teacher's load of work. Their school experiences comprise both curricular and co-curricular work: the practical school assignments relate to participation in various types of school work, both academic and otherwise. Obviously the number of class teaching periods increases and with a good number of lessons conducted during this phase, the practice teaching programme closes up. During this period the student teacher is exposed to a number of supervisors: he observes management and the working of the school, its classes, the special rooms like the library and the laboratory, and so on. He continues observing practice teaching of the teachers and prepares subsequently his observation lesson notes. The overall attainment of excellence is the aim in this final stage. Administration of achievement tests, completion of teacher's diary, preparation of school student's achievement report — are taken care of.

Criticism Lesson

Criticism lesson in the two method subjects are organised by the departments usually after the first spell of teaching but in two phases with a gap between them. These lessons are as a rule observed and supervised by the subject/method specialist together with the fellow pupil teachers. And the lessons form a part of internal assessment in practice teaching.

GROUP TWO

In an altogether different set up, in the Regional Colleges of Education, the programme for field experience of the pupil teacher takes a novel turn. The programme of practice teaching is essentially an expression of certain basic ideology in which the two colleges believe. It is held that the teacher should know that he works within a social organisation, that he has to observe, assess and help in the community development programme and that he has to acquire the required competence in teaching by identifying himself as a member of the teaching staff even from the day he associates himself with the school. The practice in teaching takes him through three phases: (i) Preparation for internship, (ii) Pre-internship, and (iii) Internship in teaching. The cumulative effect aimed at, of the experiences in three phases is a special feature of these colleges.

Preparation

The preparation for internship is intended in all senses to be very practical. The colleges lay stress on this aspect before the prospective teacher embarks on the teaching activity in actual school situation. A certain readiness has got to be created in the trainee teacher, the college holds. The pupil teacher should know:

1. what he wants to achieve in the teaching situation and how he formulates his aims, and the course of action to achieve those aims?
2. that he has to acquire control over a broad area of subject matter and adjust it to the needs of the school children,
3. that he needs to do careful planning for teaching programme and activities,
4. that he has to make himself acceptable to the teaching community and that his success depends largely upon his ability to work with others,
5. that the school in which he is placed, expects him to help maintain a high standard of personal contact, appearance, and professional efficiency and integrity.

Having these objectives in mind the colleges arrange for the necessary programme during preparatory stage. The college claims that the readiness starts even from the day orientation programme begins. Soon after the session starts, the preparation for internship, also starts. Lectures and various discourses in different forms on the theory papers are considered essential for this preparation. Besides, experience in the workshop in teaching, and in areas like Guidance, School Organisation, Health and Human Relations, Evaluation and Curriculum Planning and Teacher-Pupil Planning — for a period of about four months at the initial stage are likely to contribute much to the preparation. The whole programme thus, is geared to familiarising student teachers with various theories and principles of teaching and learning which they would require in the field. Next follows a week of orientation to teaching when student teachers get detailed information about field experiences — such as class-teaching, observation of lessons, school assignments, preparation of teaching aids, system of evaluation of internship and so on. A very important aspect of this part of the programme is coming in contact with the co-operating teacher who remains his constant guide and source of inspiration and direction throughout. A conference with the co-operating teachers and heads of schools where the student teachers are assigned for internship, help to create conditions for successful work.

Pre-internship in Teaching

The next phase in the preparation can be called pre-internship in teaching which is kept for two weeks and is placed before a student teacher goes to a co-operating school as an intern. The experiences gathered during this time are essentially geared to activities concerning classroom teaching. The theory classes in the college which have an indirect influence on the trainees are now kept suspended. Student trainees observe fully the series of demonstration lessons arranged by the faculty members either in the demonstration school attached to the college or in a few other local schools made available for the purpose. The student teacher writes the lesson notes in detail and teaches at least 4/5 lessons under the guidance and supervision of the college expert in the subject. Each lesson taught by the trainee is discussed thoroughly; all student trainees are expected to participate in the discussion.

Internship

The internship in teaching for 4 weeks, is arranged in off-campus co-operating schools. Certain criteria are used in selecting the co-operating schools: (i) The school management and the staff are willing to assist and participate in the programme of student field experience. (ii) The school selected for internship must have earned a breadth and quality in the programme that it normally follows. (iii) Student teachers find suitable housing arrangement in the vicinity of such a school. (iv) The training experience and competence of the teachers in such schools are kept in mind. (v) Provision of adequate physical facility must also be there.

Depending on the number of students such co-operating schools, may be, thirty or more spread out in neighboring 3–4 States from where the trainees come. The number of students in a school does not exceed 12/13 at a time with not more than two students specialising in a subject. This being the distribution and placement of trainees, the co-operative efforts of all personnel and more so of teachers play a decisive role in the conduct of the teaching programme. The college in a way depends so much on the continuous support and service of the personnel of the co-operating school that from planning to execution and evaluation of all experiences it is this school that renders massive help. To ensure a good programme and sound guidance the college organises a seminar where principals and cooperating teachers meet the college faculty and hold discussions regarding methods and execution of lesson plans. The informal meeting between the trainees and the co-operating teacher helps to remove many anxieties. On an average the lessons practised by each trainee number about 72; the student teacher is required to prepare weekly plan for his teaching; he gets these approved by the co-operating teacher; he is expected to try out a variety of methods of teaching as suggested by the subject department concerned. Besides the classroom teaching, the student teacher is required to (i) observe 10 lessons taught by others, (ii) complete the assessment schedule for class teaching (iii) complete written departmental assignments, (iv) take up one project either a study of co-curricular activities or a study of cumulative record or study of educational and vocational plans of secondary school students, and (v) participate in at least four school activities.

Criticism Lesson

The criticism lesson assumes a great importance. Such lessons are observed jointly by a team of the college subject/method specialist, co-operating teacher and the head of the school. The evaluation and guidance cannot be planned better than this if this is properly conducted.

GROUP THREE

There is less flexibility of approach in designing the field experience in the Colleges of Education affiliated to the university. But no inter-college comparison of how each of the three colleges under study organises the practice teaching progress is possible.

Preparation

The colleges, however, maintain, that before the student teachers are put into actual teaching situation they should have knowledge of the foundation courses in education and the related fields and experiences in the pedagogical aspect of education. This preparatory phase constitutes, (i) instruction in philosophy, psychology and history of education, (ii) instructions on general methods of teaching, (iii) demonstration lessons and observation of the same, (iv) discussion and preparation of lesson plans. There is, however, some noticeable difference seen in respect of the start as well as the duration of this preparatory phase in these university colleges.

In one college, the actual class teaching situation begins as late as November when the practice-in-teaching continues for 15 days. Each pupil-teacher teaches two lessons a day, one in each subject. Guidance in lesson planning and supervision of class room teaching by the college staff are fully available as theory classes are suspended during this period. Guidance from subject specialists is made available as far as possible. As a rule each lesson proposed to be taught by a trainee is supposed to be discussed thoroughly before it is taught. The placement of student trainees in the local five higher secondary schools may range between 15 and 25 trainees depending on the size of the school and facilities available for teaching different subjects.

In another college, practice teaching term begins as early as in August and continues for 5 weeks. Theory classes continue within the flexible time schedule. One half of the student trainees are sent for actual teaching while the other half observes them teaching. During this time each one finishes at least 15 lessons.

In order to send out students to gain the required field experience as early as in August, the college makes arrangement for about 10 days for pre-practice programme when intensive instructions are given in the methods of teaching different school subjects in addition to general methods of teaching. Mechanics of lesson planning and particularly that of unit planning are emphasised. Each student is required to draw up lesson notes and get them analysed and discussed by the method master. Demonstration lessons by the subject lecturer serve a very useful purpose to initiate students to take up classroom teaching earnestly.

In the third institution students are initiated into the field experience after they have had a month's theory work in the pedagogical aspect of education. Any need for demonstration lessons by the faculty members is not felt. But pre-teaching experience includes thorough discussion of methods of teaching the specific subjects in addition to classes on general methods. In the first term each lesson that a trainee plans to deliver, is discussed and modified by the subject incharge. All the lessons taught by the student trainee are supervised by the college staff.

Interspersed *vs.* Block Teaching

None of these three colleges organise the practice teaching experience in less than two spells of teaching. More often three spells of practice teaching seem a normal practice. Wherever two phases of teaching exist, the second spell of teaching is conducted as block teaching and students are made to teach 5 periods a day divided into two subject areas. Close guidance in lesson planning is not possible then, and each student is encouraged to write brief lesson notes for each lesson. This second phase of block teaching is intended to let students have fruitful experiences without any supervision from the college staff.

The block teaching in another institution is arranged in the third spell after the trainees have completed the second phase of practical experience for 10 days or so. They teach single lessons for another five days, thereby completing the second term quota of 15 lessons. The workload on the student teachers is heavier, as classes in all theory papers run in full swing.

In one of the colleges, of the 40 lessons the requirement set by the university, 30 lessons will have been taught before the trainees embark on the third spell of teaching. Now trainees are required to do one week's block teaching. There cannot be a fixed number of lessons to be taught. The arrangement is very much left to the Head of the practice teaching school. Student group in four batches complete this one week block teaching. Each group misses a week's class on theory because such classes can no longer remain suspended.

Criticism Lesson

The place of criticism lesson needs a careful scrutiny. Usually in these institutions such lessons are organised in both the teaching subjects but nearing the end of practice teaching term and before the student trainee takes the final and external examination in practice teaching. No planned guidance is made available for such lessons. Performances of students are observed and discussed by a group of college staff and student teachers. The method master is usually found observing the student performance and making an objective assessment before the candidate faces an external examination. These lessons form an important criterion of internal assessment and they are thoroughly discussed both by lecturers and students.

GROUP FOUR

Department of education in a large college attaches a great significance to the practice-in-teaching in a teacher education programme. They infact initiate trainees into teaching quite early. They give importance to lectures on general and particular methods of teaching quite early in the session in order to prepare the trainees for the teaching they have to do.

In a particular college (department of education) a trainee has to teach 60 lessons spread out during the whole session. The college does not have a system of organising any internship in teaching or even block teaching. Under the guidance of the method master the trainees as early as in August are put into actual contact with children and classroom teaching situation. Soon starts the class teaching usually from 10 A.M. to 1 P.M. and classes in theory papers from 2.00 P.M. to 5.00 P.M. The practice teaching programme spreads out from August to March. The placement of students in schools for teaching undergoes changes. The allocation depends on the availability of classes in schools so much so that sometimes some teachers may have to teach continuously for two terms. In the institution under review, a student completes teaching lessons in one subject before he takes up teaching in the other.

Criticism lessons are held at the end of a term in the presence of the staff members, principal and other student teachers. These lessons form a basis for recommendation of award of marks in the long run.

In another institution the student teacher is required to teach 50 lessons of which the lessons in the first semester should be between 25 to 30 and in the second semester, the rest. Equal stress is given to the preparation of the trainee through lectures and discussions. There is a place for demonstration lessons given by the method specialist. In keeping with the university requirements, the department organises the practice teaching programme in three stages:

(a) Preparation for practice-in-teaching;
(b) Practice-in-teaching in first term; and
(c) Practice-in-teaching in the second term.

(a) The preparatory period runs from 6 to 8 weeks, during which arrangements are made for instructions in theory papers, lesson planning and demonstration lessons by subject/method specialists.

(b) In the first semester the teaching continues for a month. Eight schools are used for the purpose. Student teachers, about 10 to 20 are placed in these schools, depending on the size of the school, each student is normally supposed to teach 2 lessons a day and sometimes it is three. Thus nearly 25 lessons are done when lesson plans are duly written and checked before they are taught.

(c) In the second semester, the teaching is arranged exactly in the same manner as done in the first semester. This one month's practice teaching receives full-time support and guidance as theory classes are suspended during this period.

Criticism Lesson

Unlike all other institutions, under review this department of education requires every student to deliver four criticism lessons, two in each subject arranged at the end of each semester. Lesson notes are not discussed but as performance of the student teacher is thoroughly discussed by the subject specialist and the fellow students. It helps in objective assessment of his teaching performance.

In accordance with the requirement of the Gorakhpur University, the Department of Education attached to the Degree College, Pratapgarh, U.P. places student teachers in the apprenticeship situation pretty early. But instructions in the fundamentals of teaching and methods of teaching are arranged for a month prior to sending pupils for practice teaching. They have to teach 50 lessons between August and November. During this time, theory classes in the college are held in the morning between 6-30 A.M. to 8-30 A.M. (three periods) and practice-in-teaching is held in the schools in the afternoon till 4 P.M. The Department does not organise practice teaching either in blocks or in internship form.

The practice teaching is organised in 6–8 schools; number of students placed there depends on the availability of the classes in the schools. The student begins his practice by teaching one lesson a day and later on teaching two lessons a day. No lesson is taught unless a trainee has got his lesson notes checked by the method/subject specialist.

Certain broad conclusions can be deduced now:

1. Practice-in-teaching is accepted as a very vital field experience by all the teacher training colleges. It seems to have assumed more significance than a mere adherence to a formal technicality that is, completing a number of lessons.
2. Almost all the training institutes stress the need for pre-teaching preparation for the student trainees.
3. Internship is practised in Regional Colleges only.
4. The Education Departments attached to colleges (i) do not organise teaching either as internship or in blocks,

(ii) have practice teaching arranged over 3/4 months, (iii) rarely suspend theory classes and therefore, theory classes run simultaneously with practice teaching, and (iv) have 75/80 percent of lessons normally supervised.

5. There is not a single instance where at least a certain percentage of lessons have not been supervised by the method master.
6. All institutions have provisions for criticism lesson, normally two, sometimes more than that also.

8

Supervision of Practice Teaching

Practice teaching, we have observed, is a compulsory item of all teacher training programmes and it comes usually at that phase in the sequence of the professional preparation of teachers where attempt is made to bring theory and practice together. It aims at placing the trainees in a position wherein they learn to use their theoretical knowledge effectively and in a confident manner for communicating the contents of his subject in classroom situation as well as in extra and co-curricular activities in and outside classroom situations. As such it is during this period that student teachers are expected to be actively engaged in extensive direct experiences in a school under the guidance of the staff of the teachers' college and/or co-operating school to learn the dimensions of the profession of teaching and to acquire competencies required for entering the teaching profession. Practice teaching also provides the best situation for assessing the mastery of the knowledge and skills required of an effective teacher. It has, therefore, been rightly designated as the 'Key Phase' of the total teacher education programme where attempt is made to prepare the student teacher for his multifarious responsibilities as a teacher.

Objectives of Practice-Teaching

Pires[1] in his report on 'Student Teaching Practices in Primary Teacher Training Institutions in Asia' states that the

---

1. Pires, E.A. Primary Teacher Training in Asia, Regional Office for Education in Asia, Bangkok, 1963.

objectives of student teaching can be classified into the following broad categories:

1. Objectives relating to the development in student teachers of the general ability to translate theory into practice, specially in the area of teaching methodology.
2. Objectives relating to the development of a fuller and better understanding by student teachers of the psychology of school children.
3. Objectives relating to the development in student teachers of the necessary degree of self-confidence, initiative and resourcefulness to do a creative job of teaching.
4. Objectives relating to the development in student teachers of as complete as possible an understanding of the varied roles that they will be called upon to assume when they become regular teachers by providing them with a variety of experiences related to such roles.
5. Objectives relating to the development in student teachers of a more realistic view of their tasks as teachers by familiarising them with the actual conditions and problems in the field.

The objectives of practice-teaching in secondary teacher training institutions are not different from those in primary teacher-training institutions. At the Teacher's College, Columbia University,[2] U.S.A. the student teachers as a result of laboratory experiences in relation to the Internship-in-Teaching are expected to show growth in (1) Ability to assume a teacher's role in relation to others: (a) with children (b) with adults (2) Ability to perform as a teacher in the classroom: (a) back-ground, (b) guiding learning, (c) classroom management and (3) Ability to assume a professional role: (a) professional responsibilities, (b) professional growth. These purposes similar as they are to those listed by Pires for primary teacher training institutions, are also similar to the objectives of including practice teaching in a secondary

2. Wernick, Walter, 'Teachers College, Columbia University in Evaluating Practice Teaching (A forward look at theories and practice) 39th Year Book of the Association for Student Teaching, U.S.A., 1960, pp. 67–68.

teacher training programme in India. In a study[3] of teacher training institutions in Delhi, Rajasthan, Gujarat, Jammu and Kashmir, Maharashtra, Madhya Pradesh, Punjab, Haryana and Uttar Pradesh, the objectives of keeping practice teaching in secondary teacher training programme have been recognised to be: (1) To enable the trainees to apply the knowledge of the principles and methods of teaching, (2) To prepare a ground for the actual work the trainee shall engage himself in after training, (3) To develop confidence in the trainee for meeting different instructional situations in the classroom, (4) To enable the trainee to realize the qualities demanded for success in the profession and (5) To develop in the trainee a favourable attitude towards teaching.

Need for Supervision

Few teachers are born-teachers. There is seldom seen a trainee who is perfect in the art of teaching from the very beginning and who can realize the objectives of practice teaching on his own, without the aid and guidance of the experienced master craftsman of the teaching profession. Most teachers are made. Hence during the course of his day-to-day practice-in-teaching, in order to develop the trainee into an intelligent, resourceful and effective teaching personnel, he is gradually carved out and chiselled with the aid of constant goadings, criticisms and suggestions by the college and/ or cooperating teachers who act as supervisors of practice teaching. Experts in the field of teacher education are agreed that the success and value of teaching practice depends, in a large measure, on the nature and extent of the supervision, the manner in which the supervision is undertaken and the competence of the person undertaking the supervisory task — the supervisor. The supervisor of practice teaching is the key man who can improve teaching and who can help the student teachers achieve the objectives of practice teaching. The purpose of supervision is improvement of instruction and in the student teaching situation. The supervisory organization for practice teaching and the supervisory

3. Srivastava, R.C. Evaluation of Practice Teaching in Teacher Training Institutions (Report of the Study of Evaluation of Practice Teaching in Teacher Training Institutions) Central Institute of Education, Delhi, 1970.

techniques and practices aim at bringing improvement in the instructional activity of the student teachers by familiarizing the student teachers, on the one hand, with various techniques and practical skills in teaching, and on the other, to help them to develop confidence in facing the classroom situations. Rightly, therefore, James Bryant Conant,[4] in his book 'The Education of American Teachers' argues at length that the preparation of a teacher should include a period of guided practice under the supervision of a master teacher and that this period of guided teaching should be the culminating field or laboratory activity in any teacher education programme. Practice teaching situation is an exacting ordeal. Here the student teacher has to learn to plan his lesson, to organize the contents of his teaching in a logical and coherent way and at a level suited to the intellectual and social maturity of his students, relating them to their known facts and experiences, establishing rapport with his students and motivating them to acquire new knowledge and experience and developing skills of communicating confidently and effectively with his pupils. Learning of all these is not an easy task. Practice teaching puts the student teacher in an apprenticeship situation where he must be guided and helped to develop abilities and skills to be able to function successfully as a teacher. It is the task of the supervisor to guide and help student teachers to improve their instructional activities. A sound and functional supervisory organization and programme assisted by a team of competent and committed supervisory personnel will go a long way in producing real quality teachers.

The Scene in the U.S.A.

The current scene with respect to student teaching experience designed to relate theory to practice to produce a teacher who inquires into the educative process and who is an efficient and effective classroom teacher is a spotty one. Conant[5] in his study of American teachers found that student teaching is one of the most casually conducted phases of the

4. Conant, James Bryant: The Educational of American Teachers, New York, The Macmillan Co., 1960.
5. Conant, James Bryant, *Ibid.*

enterprise. He observed that senior professors rarely want to fool with it, junior professors too often regard the supervision of student teaching as a necessary evil to be endured until promotion releases them from it, student teachers are turned over to the cooperating teachers who are vaguely aware of the programme objectives and what is expected of them by the teachers' colleges and the student teachers take the student teaching as a formality to be completed for fulfilling certification requirement. Let us examine here the situation with regard to supervision of practice teaching as it obtains in our teacher training institutions.

Programme and Practice of Supervision in India

The programme of supervision of practice teaching is arranged in all teacher training institutions in two stages:

1. Before actual classroom teaching begins.
2. During classroom teaching *i.e.*, when the student teachers are in the class, teaching their subjects to their students.

Supervision before classroom teaching begins: On campus supervision

All teacher training institutions insist that student teachers learn lesson planning. They, therefore, require their student teachers to draw lesson notes for all the lessons they propose to teach to their pupils in the class. Lesson planning demands a lot of imagination and skill on the part of the student teachers. In the beginning most student teachers consume a great deal of their time and energy in drawing a lesson note and it is not uncommon to find these lesson notes being disapproved by the subject/method specialist in the teachers' college who alone functions as supervisor at this stage of practice teaching supervision. Obviously, the student teachers need to be guided in the planning of their lessons. They have to learn to organize the contents of their teaching, formulate suitable questions of the right type to evoke right responses from the students and develop other related abilities and skills that enable them to enter and face the class successfully and with confidence. All teacher training institutions, therefore, require their student teachers to prepare their lesson notes and get them thoroughly discussed and checked up by the subject method specialist in the institution and in the light of the suggestion of these supervisors make necessary modification in their teaching plan before they are permitted to teach their lessons to their students in the class. There is, however, great diversity among teachers' colleges with regard to the number of lesson notes that must be discussed and corrected by the subject/method specialist in the institution. While institutions like Department of Education, Aligarh Muslim University prescribe a thorough discussion of 5 lesson plans of a student teacher by the subject/method specialists in Department/institution and feel that this much discussion is good enough for developing insight into planning for teaching and for learning the mechanics and techniques of lesson planning, there are institutions like Department of Education, Meerut College, Department of Education, Degree College, Pratapgarh, Lucknow University, K.P. Training College, Allahabad and many others who would have all the lesson notes drawn by a trainee discussed and checked up by the subject/method specialist in the institution and corrections incorporated by the student teacher in his lesson plan before he is allowed to teach that lesson in the class. Most of the institutions thus insist upon 100% supervision at this stage in the supervision of practice teaching by the subject/method specialist in the institution. The Regional Colleges of Education would have this supervision done by the cooperating teachers drawn from the cooperating schools for practice teaching. In the absence of research findings to suggest the optimum number of lesson plans which should be checked by the subject/method expert though it is difficult to comment on the merits or demerits of 100% or less than 100% supervision at this stage for preparation for the actual classroom teaching to follow, it appears that institutions like Aligarh Muslim University have decided on about 20% supervision at this stage for reasons of feasibility and other such considerations more than academic belief and reasoning. If planning of the lesson is a skill and has to be learned, longer practice in planning under thorough guidance and supervision is likely to be useful and beneficial to the student teacher, specially if he gets opportunity to plan for different types of lessons. However, it does not necessarily mean that 100% supervised lesson planning would automatically produce desired results.

The supervision during class teaching

The supervisory personnel

Who should supervise the off-campus teaching of the student teachers? The issue is beset with varying viewpoints. MacNair[6] Committee recommended that the primary responsibility of supervision during the school practice period should rest with the college tutor or lecturer but during the period of continuous school practice, in other words, during the block teaching period, it should be the responsibility of the head and the teachers of the practising school. D'Souza and Chatterji[7] plead for a partnership role between the college and the school supervisory personnel at all phases of practice teaching supervision but put the responsibility in matters of supervision of practice teaching primarily on the teachers' college faculty. James Bryant Conant[8] on the other hand, holds, altogether a different point of view. Knowing fully well that training college lecturers are often out of contact with the schools and the day-to-day business of teaching, he strongly advises that the guided teaching must always be done under the supervision and care of the master teachers in the schools. According to him these senior practising school teachers are the best persons, qualified and suited to do this type of work because they are on the job and can provide real apprenticeship situation and training for the student teachers in their process of becoming efficient and effective classroom teachers. Both these points of view are reflected in the supervisory practices of our teacher training institutions, but whereas Conant's advice seems to be more feasible and convincing, the MacNair Committee[9] recommendations are more popular and put into practice in greater number of institutions, perhaps because good teachers in the schools are not common enough and the best would not be able to

---

6. MacNair Report: Teacher and Youth Leaders, Ministry of Education, H.M.S.O., London, 1944.
7. D'Souza, Austin A, Chatterji, J.N. Training for Teaching in India and England, Orient Longmans, 1956, pp. 115–139.
8. Conant, James Bryant, *ibid*.
9. MacNair Report: *ibid*.

explain what made them good teachers. Then, most teachers tend to get into a rut and out of touch with new methods and ideas.

The organization and management of supervision of class teaching during off-campus school practice in all teacher training institutions/departments except in the two Regional Colleges of Education studied, is the main responsibility of the coordinator of practice teaching, who is generally a senior member of the staff of the teachers' college/department. In these colleges/departments whole faculty whether or not they are subject specialists, is involved in the supervision of off-campus student teaching, and the major responsibility for the guidance and supervision of student teaching is assumed by the teachers' colleges themselves, both for off-campus as well as on-campus student teaching and Conant's advice that guided teaching be done under the supervision and care of the master teachers in the schools has gone, in these colleges mostly unheeded. But unlike the supervision of off-campus school practice which may be done by a non-subject teacher of the college, the supervision of on-campus teaching, as we have seen in this section earlier, is the responsibility of the subject specialists in the college. However, this supervision is confined mainly to discussion and checking up of lesson notes prepared by the student teachers. The Regional Colleges of Education function more on the lines suggested by Conant.[10] They employ three groups of personnel for guiding and supervising the Internship activities of student teachers. These three groups of personnel are:

1. Subject teachers from the college subject department concerned.
2. Pedagogy experts from the college education department.
3. Cooperating teachers and headmasters/principals of the cooperating schools.

And, the major burden of guiding and supervising the off-campus teaching and other field experiences falls on the personnel from the cooperating schools — the cooperating teachers and the cooperating headmasters/principals of the schools. The cooperating teachers provide to the student

10. Conant, James Bryant, *Ibid.*

teachers, time table for class teaching, help them in preparing outline of the teaching scheme by selecting suitable and appropriate contents of his teaching, discuss each lesson of the student teacher, check it and suggest modifications, supervise his day-to-day teaching, and write comments and suggestions on each lesson in the light of the criteria for observations and evaluation of class teaching. The cooperating teachers are assisted in their supervision work by the subject as well as pedagogy experts from the Regional Colleges when they in turn visit the schools for practice teaching for 2/3 days and are available both to the cooperating teachers and student teachers for any help and guidance. The supervision of the on-campus teaching, in these Regional Colleges is the shared responsibility of teachers in the subject departments and education department of the college.

The arrangement for supervision

With a clearcut definition of the functions and responsibilities of the personnel engaged in the supervision of student teaching (Internship-in-Teaching) in the Regional Colleges of Education it is not difficult to make suitable arrangement for the supervision of both on-campus as well as off-campus teaching of student teachers. The on-campus teaching is supervised by the teachers in the subjects and education department of these colleges and as this teaching is arranged in the Demonstration School attached to the colleges and in a few local schools and the college faculty being available for supervisory work, each of the four lessons taught by a trainee is looked into and thoroughly discussed by the college experts from both subjects and education departments. In these discussions the student teachers are expected to participate actively in order to learn and appreciate their strong and weak teaching points. The supervision of off-campus teaching needs, greater planning because teaching at this phase is done in the cooperating schools located far away from the college campus and under the major supervisory control of the cooperating teachers and headmasters of the cooperating schools. In order that the supervisory personnel from the cooperating schools understand and appreciate the significance of the Internship programme and their part in it, these colleges organize a seminar of the principals/headmasters and cooperating teachers to orient them about their expected role in the programme and also with the new and established methods and techniques of class teaching and supervision. With sufficient funds, facilities and resources at their disposal, the Regional Colleges are able to arrange a programme/scheme of supervision through which 70% to 80% of the lessons taught by a student teacher are supervised, and of these 70% to 80% supervised lessons, 25% to 30% lessons get supervised by the college supervisors from the subject and the education departments and the rest *i.e.*, 45% to 50% lessons are supervised by the cooperating teachers who are experienced subject teachers in the school setting and who have had guidance and orientation from the subject and pedagogy experts from the Regional College, both in respect of teaching methods and techniques of supervision.

The arrangement for supervision of the off-campus teaching in colleges and departments, other than the Regional College is not so well defined and varies from institution to institution. It also is beset with problems of a different kind. Unlike, in the Regional Colleges practice teaching in all other teacher training institutions is organized in local schools selected mostly from amongst those in the vicinity of the training institution. Most of these institutions suffer from handicaps of financial and other resources. The present condition of staffing and organization in these institutions is though not quite satisfactory yet they in their own way and belief attempt to arrange a programme of supervision of practice teaching to realize the purposes of supervision. In these institutions supervision of actual classroom teaching is the responsibility of all the members of the academic staff of the institution. But the supervisory arrangement varies from institution to institution, for they within their own limitations try to create conditions in which student teachers teaching a subject are exposed as far as possible to maximum supervision of their teaching by the subject/method specialist from the institution who had oriented them with the mechanics and techniques of lesson planning. These are some of the practices of arranging supervision of student teaching:

1. Assigning a supervisor to each practice teaching school. These supervisors are generally called regular supervisor and are in the main responsible for the general guidance and

supervision of student teachers put under their charge. The number of student teachers under a supervisor, in this arrangement usually ranges from 8 to 12, and they may constitute a very heterogeneous group so far as their teaching subjects are concerned and in many a case it may so happen that the supervisor may not get an opportunity to supervise the teaching of a student teacher of his own subject speciality. To overcome this situation, these institutions may also organize rotation supervision so that student teachers are exposed to the supervision by several supervisors of practice teaching. During rotation supervision attempt is made to draw such a scheme/schedule of supervision in which the subject/method specialist from the college/department gets at least one chance to observe and guide the student teacher teaching the subject of his own speciality. The purpose in arranging for such a supervision is that the student teacher may not only receive general supervision but also get guidance on matter and aspects specifically related to the subject of his teaching from those who know the subject and are also responsible for the methods of teaching of that subject in the college and constitute the subject specialist group. The frequency of rotation supervision, however, is not the same in the institutions which try to have this type of arrangement for supervision of practice teaching. Some institutions insist that supervisors of practice teaching should rotate from one school to another on a daily, bi-weekly or weekly basis while others may remain content with organizing one or at the most two rotation supervisions during the whole practice teaching term.

2. Under this arrangement of practice teaching supervision instead of assigning one permanent supervisor for a group of student-teachers placed in a school, the college arranges a system of team supervision in which a team of two or more teachers is given the responsibility of supervising the student teaching of student teachers in a school. The team of supervisors may or may not rotate from one school to another. In the institutions where supervision of practice teaching is arranged in this manner, effort is made to classify the training college teachers into the categories like: (1) Science and Mathematics, (2) Languages (3) Social Sciences and one member from each of these categories is drawn to form a team of supervisors who may continue to visit a school

on a regular and permanent basis for the whole duration of the practice teaching term or may rotate from one school to another depending on the type of arrangement made, keeping in mind the available facilities of movement and location of the schools for practice teaching.

Supervision of criticism lessons

The teacher training institution may require the student teachers to deliver a criticism lesson in each of his teaching subjects. These criticism lessons may be arranged after a student teacher has taught more than ten lessons in a subject or has completed the first spell of practice teaching, but the general practice is to arrange these lessons after the student teacher has taught about twenty supervised lessons in each of his subjects and is thus near finishing/completing the practical teaching requirement of the teacher education programme. The purpose of arranging the criticism lesson is three-fold: (1) To provide an opportunity to student teachers to plan and execute his lesson in the class without any aid and guidance from the supervisor of practice teaching and thus to show his potentialities as a skilled and effective teacher of his subject, (2) To provide an opportunity for clinical supervision of the student teacher's teaching by a group of teachers and/or students and (3) To assess the attainment of the various teaching skills and abilities by the student teacher. The arrangement for the supervision of criticism lessons, therefore, is generally different from the arrangement made for supervision of day-to-day teaching of the student teacher where the main purpose of supervision is to aid the development of skills and abilities of student teachers to teach his subject. But here also the practices differ from institution to institution. In institutions like Lady Irwin College, New Delhi and the Central Institute of Education, Delhi the criticism lessons are looked into, observed and supervised by the permanent regular supervisor of the student teachers who may be a non-subject specialist alongwith a group of student teachers teaching the subject in the school, but in most other institutions the arrangement for supervision of these lessons is made in such a manner that if not the whole college faculty and the student teachers teaching the subject participate in the supervisory activity, at least the subject/method specialist, alongwith a few faculty members and student teachers teaching the subject in question observe and offer comments and suggestions on the teaching of the student teacher who delivers the criticism lesson. This clinical supervision by the group is considered to function better for realizing the purposes for which criticism lessons are organised and helps to improve teaching skills of the student teacher as well as create conditions for a more objective assessment of student teacher's performance as a teacher.

Supervision by the Subject / Method Specialist

It would, no doubt, be the most desirable and ideal situation in which a student teacher is exposed to the supervision of his teaching by the subject method specialist but the staff position in the teacher training institutions/departments and the manner in which these institutions are organized, create conditions for supervision that is far from the ideal. In the circumstances some institutions have been shaken in their belief and they have begun to feel that it is neither necessary nor feasible that all the lessons taught by a trainee in a particular subject be supervised only by the subject method specialist on the college staff. However, most of the institutions still uphold the merit of 100% supervision of student teaching by the subject method expert and work for an arrangement for supervision in that direction, though they are not able to manage an arrangement in many a case for even 50% supervision by the subject specialist and most of the institutions have to be content with much less supervision ranging from less than 50% to 30% of supervision by subject teachers.

The nature and content of supervision

When the major share of responsibility for the guidance and supervision of student teaching, is assumed by the teachers' colleges themselves and Conant's advice that guided teaching be done under the supervision and care of the master teachers in the school has gone mostly unheeded and when there has not been much change in the pattern of appointing the teachers' college faculty, the student teachers tend to receive a general supervision from the college supervisors who are often neither subject method specialists nor have been active school teachers of the subject for years. In a study in 1962 by Srivastava,[11] it was reported that these supervisors mostly offered descriptive type of criticism, though constructive type of criticism was the most desirable one. These remarks related to: (1) general personality bearing of the student teachers (2) questioning, (3) blackboard work, (4) class management and discipline, and (5) overall impression. The supervisors seldom critically appreciated the student teacher's knowledge of the subject and the order of its presentation to the students. The study also reported that the supervisors failed to supervise all the lessons taught by a trainee and in many a case not more than 25% of the lessons were supervised. The percentage of lessons supervised by the subject method specialist varied from 5% to 25% of the lessons taught by a student teacher. Several reasons for lack of proper supervision were stated. They were: the faculty staffing pattern resulting into shortage or non-availability of the subject method specialist, uneven distribution of teaching subject among the student teachers, lack of time and too many lessons to be supervised in a class period, defective time table, etc. Pires,[12] as early as in 1952 reported some similar difficulties in conducting a satisfactory supervisory programme of practice teaching. Among the difficulties reported the most important were the following:

1. Excessive number of students.
2. Scatter of student teachers in a large number of schools in different parts of the city coupled with difficulties of conveyance of members of the staff.
3. Other courses like the J.S.T.C., the M.Ed. being conducted in the same institution with the help of the same staff, resulting in an insufficiency of supervisors.
4. Inadequacy of practising schools.
5. Compulsory arrangement of a large number of lessons — sometimes as many as six in a single period.

---

11. Srivastava, R.C. 'Improving the supervision of practice teaching in Trainee Colleges'. The progress of Education, Vol. XXXVII, No. 3 Oct. 1962.
12. Pires, E.A. Better Teacher Education, University Press, Delhi, 1958, pp. 109.

Rastogi[13] studied in 1969 the supervision of practice teaching of the students of B.Ed. Course through Correspondence and reported that the supervision of student teaching was mostly of a general nature and the supervisors in observing and guiding teaching of the student teachers gave high importance to development of the lesson, question and response technique and use of blackboard and low importance to subject matter, assignment in a subject, recapitulation, narration and reading and the use of the material aid. The situation has not been very different from what it was in 1969 or even earlier in 1962 in most of the training colleges except that the Regional Colleges of Education and a few progressive teacher training institutions have recognised the need and usefulness of a more give-and-take relationship between the training institution and the school and also the role of the subject method specialist in developing positive attitude towards teaching as a profession, and in the improvement of the student teaching performance.

In the context of the findings of these studies it is proposed that the supervision of student teaching be the joint responsibility of the college faculty represented mainly by the method masters and the school teachers and the major share of responsibility in this enterprise should rest with the school teachers. It is so proposed because the supervision of student teaching requires more than simply the art of teaching. To guide and appraise the student teacher, the supervisor must obviously have a more thorough understanding of his field and of such educational disciplines as psychology and such a supervisor can generally be available mainly in a college faculty. Therefore, the school teacher should be assisted in his work of supervision of student teacher by the college supervisor of student teaching. Frequent conferences and consultations between them will not only help relate them to practice, but will also help the student teacher to improve his performance in a realistic school setting. The student teaching will continue to fall far short of its potentialities until the methods specialists and the successful school teachers are given the highest status in the faculty and are

13. Rastogi, K.G. Supervision of Practice Teaching (Report of the study of the supervision of practice of teaching of students of B. Ed. course through correspondence), Central Institute of Education, Delhi, 1969.

held responsible for organizing supervision and carrying out of the student teaching programme.

9

Evaluation of Practice Teaching

Importance of Evaluation in Student/Practice Teaching

Evaluation is an important and useful concomitant of all educational programmes. It is recognised as an integral part of the teaching learning process and much emphasis is placed on the function of self-evaluation as an aid to continuous personal and professional development. In the Examination ridden society and educational system, where the merit of a person is judged on the basis of marks or grades he has secured in the examination, how far have the modern concept of evaluation been put into practice should be of concern to those charged with the responsibility of evaluating educational and teaching standards in schools. It is the bane of our educational system that evaluation occupies a key position. The teacher training institutions are no exception to this rule. The student teachers are motivated primarily by the marks or grades they are going to get in the examination. As in other areas, evaluation is an inseparable part of all learning in student/practice teaching. The success of the student/practice teaching programmes and practices depend on how these experiences are evaluated. If the student teachers are assured that everyone who goes through the student teaching experience, passes, the student/practice teaching programme is bound to end in a formality and cause the development of an indifferent attitude towards this phase of the programme. Since student teaching is the capstone of the teacher education programme, it is at this phase that an honest look should be taken at each would-be teacher. The standards and exceptations for the evaluation of teaching should be firmly rooted in the student/practice teaching phase, for it is these, that will be carried over into teaching itself. If the standard of the evaluation of student/practice teaching is high and the principle governing student teaching evaluation is such that it is continuous, cooperative and objective and if it is done in terms of clearly defined and clearly understood purposes, it will not only strengthen the security of the student teachers, but at the same time will also help each of these individuals to be constantly critical of his own teaching.

Definition of Evaluation

Evaluation is a process to determine how well a task is being done. It implies two factors: a goal to be attained and a standard to determine the quality of the attainment. That is, there is an objective, an attempt to attain it, a look-see to determine what has been done, a recording of what is accomplished, and some suggestions for change for the 'next-time'. In the evaluation of student teaching, the college supervisor and the cooperating teacher observe the activity and the environment, compare what is seen against the standard, judge the value of what is observed and compared and plan for recording and reappraisal.

Why Evaluate?

The primary purpose of evaluation is to help the student teacher understand and accept himself and to set for himself realistic professional goals. Another purpose is to help college faculty to assess the college programme and to lay the basis for its improvement. Evaluation serves as a guide to students in their first teaching experience, and helps in their placement when they are ready for inservice appointment. The student has a right to know how he is doing, and the great value comes from his knowing how to analyze his own strengths and weaknesses so that he can capitalize on his potential abilities. Evaluation creates in the student teacher a desire to change, the willingness to admit his own limitations and to enjoy his own success. It enables him to see what is happening in his classroom and why it is happening. In sharing in the evaluative process, he gains a clear idea of what is expected and how well he is achieving.

Beginning of Student/Practice Teaching Evaluation

From the beginning of the professional preparation of teachers, practice-in-teaching or student teaching has been an essential part of the teacher-education curriculum. Cyrus Peirce[1] the first principal of the first normal school in the United States in Lexington, Massachusetts, as early as in 1839 included student teaching/practice-in-teaching and governing a model or experimental school among the studies for the professional education of teachers. For Peirce,[2] the first principle in evaluation of practice-in-teaching was that one who evaluates it should understand the purposes of the learning or experiences to be evaluated. He laid stress on the continuous evaluation of student teaching and involved student teachers in the evaluation process. Evaluation of student teaching took a leap forward when self criticism was encouraged and foundations for a higher level of evaluation was laid by Edward A. Sheldon,[3] Principal of the Oswego Normal School for the utilization of the student's ability to criticize himself.

Relation between Theory and Practice of Evaluation

Theory of evaluation do affect practices. The theory has significance as it relates to practice-in-teaching and practice teaching programmes generally and specifically. It determines the principles and processes of evaluation and helps in devising evaluative instruments and procedure and in properly placing the responsibility for evaluation. It is important, therefore, that all those concerned with student teaching evalua-

---

1. Peirce, Cyrus: reported in Arthur O. Norton: The First Normal School in America, Cambridge, Massachussets, Harvard University Press, 1926, p. 1.
2. Peirce, Cyrus: *Ibid.*
3. Sheldon, Edward A. in Ned H. Dearborn 'The Oswego Movement in American Education, New York, Bureau of Publications, Teachers College, Columbia University, 1925, p. 39.

tion know why and how to evaluate. The procedure of evaluation should be rooted in purposeful functions. These functions should be understood clearly by persons responsible for evaluation in order that they can more ably guide others in group and self appraisals, respond more intelligently and confidently to those who may inquire about the nature, function or quality of their evaluation programme and help the student teacher understand the significance of theory in determining the nature and function of evaluation.

Importance of Evaluation for Student Teacher

Evaluation, in other words, the making of plans and judgments in terms of desired goals contributes to the student teacher's self-realization as a teacher in terms of characteristics, competencies and responsibility for self-growth through self analysis of his effectiveness in guiding learning. The major function of student teaching evaluation generally agreed upon is that it should contribute to the improvement and development of the student teaching and the pre-student teaching programmes and to the personal, professional and socio-civic growth of student teachers.

Relation of Practice Teaching Evaluation and Quality of Practice Teaching

Practice teaching evaluation methods and procedures are related to the quality of practice teaching and the attitude student teachers may have towards practice teaching programmes and practices. Studies by Corrigan and Grisword[4]; Nagle,[5] Sandgren and Schmidt,[6] and Triosi[7] provide evidence that student teaching is an effective means for

4. Corrigan, Dean and Grisword, Kenneth: 'Attitude changes of Student Teachers', Journal of Educational Research, 1963.
5. Nagle, L. Marshall: 'Some Effects of Student-Teaching Pattern upon Professional, Attitudes', Journal of Educational Research, 52: 355–57, May, 1959.
6. Sandgren, Duane L, Schmidt, Louis G.: 'Does Practice-Teaching Change Attitude towards Teaching' Journal of Educational Research, 47: 673–80, May, 1956.
7. Triosi, Nicholas F.: 'The Effect of Student Teaching upon Student Teachers Objectives and their relation to Achievement and Attitudes towards Children' Doctoral Thesis, Pennyslavania State University, 1959, Dissertation Abstract 20: 509 No. 1, 1959.

changing the attitudes of prospective teachers towards youth, towards the teaching profession and towards their day-to-day classroom activities. They found that attitudes of student-teachers improved during the period of time in which the guided student teaching was taken and recommended that a person planning to teach should be guided and properly evaluated in the classroom experience prior to assuming independent responsibility as a teacher. These studies and their own observations have helped the teacher educators to recognise that evaluation affects the quality of teaching and learning in many ways. Evaluation procedures may bring about in the student teachers a sharpened insight into and understanding of the self and of others and it may thus bring about improved relationship between the students and the supervising teachers, between the college and the practice teaching or the cooperating schools and of all those who are involved in the evaluation process. Such understanding and relationships derive from continuous and cooperative evaluation mechanisms and are likely to affect the quality of practice teaching. However, the maximum impact of evaluation in teacher education has not yet been felt.

Research related to Practice Teaching Evaluation

The general status of research relating to the evaluation of practice-teaching cannot until recently be regarded favourably. Genuine research in educational evaluation did not begin until around 1905. One of the earliest pieces of research concerning the evaluation of teaching was done by J.F. Merriam in 1905. Merriam used a sample of 1185 normal school graduates in an attempt to show the relationship between professional scholarship and teaching ability. He concluded from the extremely low correlation that normal school scholarship had a negligible relation to future ability in teaching. The development of the Ohio Teaching Record at the Ohio State University in 1939 was another unique contribution to the process of evaluation of teaching. In 1945, a sub committee of the American Association of the Colleges for Teacher Education was charged with the responsibility of the accreditation standards governing student teaching. The committee suggested that (1) the programme of evaluation be continuous and cooperative with participation by the students and the members of the faculty, (2) evaluation should not be concerned with specific techniques or patterns and (3) emphasis should be placed on the student's ability to use knowledge, understanding and generalizations as guides to action. In India, in 1963 and again in 1970 Srivastava[8] carried out a survey of the evaluation of practice teaching in teacher training institutions and has highlighted the divergent practices prevalent among the various teacher training colleges affiliated to universities in north India and in addition has offered some valuable suggestions to make evaluation more objective, valid and reliable.

Need for Setting up Goals for Practice Teaching and its Evaluation

An effective programme of evaluation of the teaching-learning process will embody in general the goals and principles basic to the programme of teacher education. The objectives of the teacher education programme, therefore, are the main sources for obtaining purposes and principles of the evaluation and of its student teaching programme. It is important that a student grows because of the evaluative process, not despite it. Therefore, when the preparation of the student is for wholesome, satisfying and productive life activities as well as for instructional or supervisory assignments in the schools it is important that goals and working principles be set up to make such product possible.

Objectives of Practice Teaching Evaluation

Student teaching involves a variety of personnel, interpretations and functions. If there is to be harmony, understanding, on-going growth and development certain commonly accepted goals and principles must serve as guides in the evaluation of student teaching. Where schools and colleges dedicate themselves to a common purpose and both feel the responsibility for continued growth or for the improvement of teaching-learning situation, the need arises for clearly

8. Srivastava, R.C. 'Evaluation of Practice-Teaching in Teacher-Training Institution' (Report of a research project) published by the Central Institute of Education, Delhi in the Series C.I.E. Studies in Education and Psychology, 1970.

stated goals and working principles. These serve as guides in maintaining understandings and positive working relationships and in securing the realization of the philosophy of teacher education or the purpose for which it exists. As stated in Chapter VIII, the objectives of keeping practice teaching in a teacher education programme are more or less the same in secondary and primary teacher training institutions both in India and abroad and the purposes basic to the evaluation of the student and his teaching generally agreed upon are the following:

1. To inform the student teacher of his progress.
2. To guide him in areas needing further development.
3. To help to extend his horizons into areas not necessarily a requirement in student teaching.
4. To clarify the thinking of all concerned with the student teacher regarding the quality of his work.
5. To establish the importance of self-evaluation to the extent that continuous in-service education may evolve.
6. To arrive at a grade or final statement of his present teaching experience.
7. To seek continuous ways of improving the student teaching programme.

These are the general objectives of student teaching and in listing these we are only stating the obvious. However, to list the specific objectives is practically impossible. Some of the basic competencies that are emphasised in evaluating the student teacher's growth are (1) his ability to generalise from his experiences (2) his ability to determine specific procedures from his generalizations, (3) the insight that he demonstrates in meeting, in varying degrees, responsibility for the guidance of learning experiences, and (4) the ability of the student to evaluate himself and prescribe productive improvement measures. In other and more simple words it can be said that evaluation in practice teaching should serve the following purposes:

1. To identify some of the skills, competencies and qualities considered basic to effective teaching.
2. To aid the student teacher to become aware of which competencies have been achieved and which are still to be achieved.
3. To enable all the persons engaged in guiding the stu-

dent teachers to provide the recognition, specific experience and suggestions which can aid the student teacher to continuously expand his competencies as a teacher.

4. To help in arriving at a final grade or statement of his present teaching experiences.

Principles of Practice Teaching Evaluation

The principles of practice teaching evaluation have been derived as a result of need and of actual usage. Although these principles have not been validated against any theoretical framework, they have been largely accepted and put into practice. These principles are:

— Goals are cooperatively established by all concerned with the student's progress.
— Cooperative inquiry and action are basic in the evaluative process.
— Growth of the student, as well as his present performance, is the measure of achievement.
— Concern of evaluation is with potentials and processes, as well as with outcome.
— Several different student teaching experiences for each student are essential for continued self-evaluation and critical thinking.
— Individual conference follows as soon as possible after the supervisor's visit.
— Student teaching group conferences or seminars foster critical thinking and analysis.
— Determination of the final grade for the student's present experience is the responsibility of the college supervisors but this decision is based on the cooperative evaluation of all concerned with supervision and guidance of student teaching.
— A systematic record for each student experiences during practice teaching is maintained and used in evaluating growth or for planning further experiences.
— Continuous evaluation is essential to growth in student teaching.

The basic principle governing evaluation, whether it be in the Regional Colleges of Education, the Department of Education of a university or in a training college affiliated to a university or the State department of education is that the evaluation of all experiences relating practice-in-teaching/ internship-in-teaching — class teaching and sessional work/ field experiences should be continuously and jointly evaluated on a cooperative basis by all those concerned with the planning, execution, guidance and supervision of practice teaching which suggests that in most teachers' colleges student teachers are also associated with the work of evaluating practice teaching, except a few colleges like Degree College, Partapgarh which are against associating student teachers in the evaluation activity.

Content and Method of Practice Teaching Evaluation

What is to be evaluated in Practice-in-Teaching? Answer to this question demands that the functions and roles of the teacher be defined in terms of purposes focussed on developing basic teaching competencies and criteria. It also demands establishment of well defined standard for rating student-teachers so that ratings are arrived at and interpreted objectively by person concerned. The methods and procedures of evaluation depend upon one's concept of the functions of evaluation. The instruments and contents used for evaluation purposes accordingly vary in kind and extent of use. Such instruments as rating scales, diaries, logs, records of scholastic achievements, personal data records, anecdotal records, observation forms and questionnaires etc. alongwith personal interviews, individual or group conferences are often used for evaluating student teaching. But the colleges make their own selection of those instruments and use them in their own ways accordingly to their needs — some using it regularly and systematically and some putting these to not so active use.

The Contents of Practice Teaching Evaluation

The objectives of practice teaching should get translated in the contents and methods of practice teaching evaluation. For, it is through the contents and methods of evaluation that an assessment can be made of the extent to which the objectives of practice teaching have been realized by the student teachers. And, as the evaluation takes place on the evidence that is furnished by the student's behaviour in given situations, the objectives of practice teaching are stated on the behaviour level.

Class teaching and practical sessional work/field experiences are generally used as two main criteria for evaluating the achievement of objectives of practice teaching, which at least in respect of class teaching, in most colleges are analysed and stated on the behavioural level. Between the two criteria, class teaching is accorded usually more weightage than the sessional or field work. But some institutions may assess the student teacher's performance on the basis of his achievement in class teaching alone and may not give any weightage to sessional work in their evaluation scheme. Knowledge of the teaching subject, presentation of subject matter, lesson planning, conduct of classroom routine, skill in the use of teaching devices and techniques, class management and discipline and personality qualities are the various groups of items that are looked into while making the assessment on student's performance in class teaching in all the institutions. The list of items under sessional work which may or may not be directly considered in evaluating practice teaching is, however, long and varied. The contents of sessional work evaluation may be classified under, (A) Theory work, (B) Practical School Assignment, (C) Visual Education and Craft, (D) Psychology practicals, (E) Extra-Curricular activities and may include specific items like: class tests, essays, term papers, participation in tutorials, analysis of text-book, study of an aspect of the school, analysis of question paper, construction of achievement test, conducting the examination, case study, action research, projects and field work including subject clubs, class magazine, school register, preparation of charts, pictures, models, craft and scrap book; game and sports, dramatic and music, debates and symposiums, physical education (P.T.), organization of tours and trips, community living, scouting and first aid, and gardening. But not all of these sessional work items form part of practice teaching evaluation in a college. The colleges may select a group of items in one year and change them with others next year or after. The teacher training institutions generally consider the class teaching and sessional work required to be put in by a student teacher to be mutually complementary and suggest that balanced weightage be given to these in terms of marks and time assigned to those in the programme, but desire that these sessional work activities should be so chosen that they support and improve the class teaching performance of the student teachers. Many of these sessional work activities, it shall be seen are not related to class teaching, though these may to some extent contribute to producing a wholesome, satisfying and liberally educated teacher. In the view of the present writer, therefore, some sessional work activities though may be included in a teacher education programme but they need not be clubbed together with practice teaching, which should be in the main concerned with improving the skill in class teaching. Evaluation of practice teaching should be done only on the basis of the level of achievement reached in teaching the subject matter in the class, and if, the sessional work activities are also evaluated the statement of achievement in sessional work and teaching/practice-in-teaching, must always be shown separately so that student teachers not good enough in class teaching may not be declared as passed in practice-in-teaching, because of their better performance/achievement in sessional work activities.

Methods, Procedures and Techniques of Practice Teaching Evaluation

The student teachers' performance in practice teaching is evaluated either wholly internally with the aid of college faculty and also sometimes with the aid of cooperating teachers as well or wholly externally by the examiners appointed for the purpose by the examining agencies or it is evaluated by a combination of internal-external evaluation system. The system of evaluating practice teaching in vogue in the teacher training institution can be broadly and conveniently grouped into five types *viz.* 100% internal, more internal than external, 50% internal — 50% external, more external than internal and 100% external. Earlier studies[9,10] on this subject have suggested the trend in teacher training institutions towards

9. Srivastava, R.C. 'Evaluating Student-Teaching and its Effect on the Trainees' Journal of Education and Psychology, Vol. XXI. No. 1, April 1963.
10. Srivastava, R.C. Evaluation of Practice-Teaching in Teacher-Training Institutions (*Ibid*).

having some system of internal assessment and to have a combined internal-external system. There is no doubt that the educational administrators and the University Grants Commission have prepared a scheme for introducing 100% internal evaluation system in all the universities offering professional as well as non-professional courses of studies but teacher educators and student teachers by and large do not want to give weightage to internal assessment any more than 50% of the total marks assigned for practice teaching. They find the internal assessment quite often to be biased and lenient and in practice based on vague memory and without making any reference to records that might have been kept by the evaluating personnel. Although in making the internal assessment, attempt is made to reach a consensus in joint meetings of the personnel evaluating the performance of a student teacher, but the long interval at which the meetings are held (in most cases the meetings are held only once at the fag end of the session and is held not more than once in a year) and the manner in which the consensus is reached, can hardly do justice to the internal evaluation system. During his visits to various teacher training institutions and also as teacher in several teacher's colleges in the last more than three decades, the author cannot recall a single instance in which the evaluating personnel, may he be a college supervisor or the cooperating teacher, writing out and presenting a detailed report about a student teacher's strong and weak points for discussions in such meetings like the way it is reported to be done in Teachers' College, Columbia University. At the Teachers' College, each report is read to the group by the staff member who writes it. Each member attempts to fix a mark for the student and uses the report as a guide to discussion. The report[11] normally reads like this:

'Miss J ended her student teaching in, what one may call for lack of a better term, 'a blaze of glory'. The expression is apropos when one contrasts her last week and a half with the rest of her student teaching period, especially the first several weeks . . . originally in another classroom situation but because she was uncomfortable there, a switch was made

11. Evaluating Student Teaching, 39th Year Book of the Association for Student-Teaching, U.S.A., 1960.

on November fifth. She was then haunted with sickness which caused her to be absent more than was ideal for a person trying to get into the routines and teaching of a relatively new classroom situation. An abnormally heavy schedule of courses at the college and. . .(her) unwillingness to forego the pleasantries of her social life probably did not help much either. Whatever the cause, it was plain that. . .(her) teaching, while adequate, lacked spark and drive. That is, until just recently. With examination week almost finished,. . .(she) took over the reins of the class, and it was then that the potential we knew that resided in her manifested itself. She began to follow through on suggestions made. She definitely began to assume the teacher's role in her expectations of children's learnings and behaviour. She has shown initiative in trying new ways of teaching. She has planned and implemented an excellent unit on weather and correlated and integrated all subjects with her supervising teacher's long term plans. She often took the lead from the children in her presentation of her lessons. With experience she should become expert at this. She has learned to speak slowly in giving directions and is now working on not trying to talk over the voices of the children. (She early established rapport with them.) Miss J needs to develop more interesting means of motivating the children. Presently she is too matter-of-fact in her presentations. She also needs to become more aware of the physical surroundings such as lighting, facing children away from the windows, etc. She is becoming more aware of peripheral actions on the part of the children who are supposed to be giving their attention to other matters. With more experience she should have this under control. Also as she gains security, she should make more extensive use of judicious praise which she was just beginning to do rather well. These last suggestions are not to detract from the really commendable job she did these last two weeks. Had she but been able to do as well earlier, she, no doubt, would have shown much growth in these areas as well.

What would you have given this girl for a final mark?

'B+'

'B+'

'B+'

"B—' or 'C+' depending upon other circumstances
'C+' I had one like that and after discussing with the coordinator I changed it from a "B—' to a "C+'

I think she should be in the 'B' range because she showed she was capable of 'A' work which lots of people are not capable of ever showing, I gave her a 'B'.

Unless a report like the above is presented and discussed and that too more frequently in meetings of the concerned staff, the system of internal assessment will leave much that is desired and till that situation is created and put into practice the present author feels that the internal evaluation system should be supported with an external examination of practice teaching which carries weightage if not more at least equal to that of the internal assessment. Theoretically and from the academic point of view, the system of wholly internal assessment is the most sound and desirable one, but in view of the student teachers perceiving a lot of the element of subjectivity, prejudice and bias in such a system and the teacher educators reporting the development of unfavourable attitude towards practice teaching, both in the wholly internal as well as in the wholly external system, it is not feasible at present to introduce the system of wholly internal or external assessment of practice teaching and wherever such a system is in vogue, it has seriously considered for a change for a mixed internal-external system, with a provision that there is a limit fixed on the external examiners for seeing not more than one lesson in a class period, and that each lesson is observed by all the examiners at the same time.

Another observation that is worth considering is the fact that the examining agencies do not define or outline the scheme of marks distribution over the contents of class teaching evaluation, and the institutions are free whether or not to develop a scheme. Most of the institutions in both internal as well as external system make an overall assessment of the student's performance. They do not have a scheme of distributing marks over the contents of class teaching evaluation and there is no common pattern of marks distribution in the few institutions which have devised a distinct scheme of marks distribution over these items, although there is more or less an agreement on the various items that should go into class teaching evaluation. In order that these items are evaluated properly and objectively it is necessary that there is a distinct system of distribution of examination marks over each of these items of practice teaching, for in its absence, there is every likelihood of the evaluation being vague, inadequate and shaded with the element of subjectivity, which in turn is bound to cause not only dissatisfaction and grumbling among student teachers but also deterioration in their standard of performance in teaching. However, even this specification and distinct distribution of marks over the specified items will not do away with the element of subjectively completely but it will certainly help to narrow down the scope of bias and vagueness and this is what can be most useful and practicable at this stage.

In any programme of improvement of education evaluation plays a very important role. The system of evaluation should be valid, reliable and should aid the student teacher's growth. But there is no ready made solution as to how it can bring this about. There is a need to pooling together of all the work that has been done or will be done in the area of student teaching evaluation to evolve a purposeful, free from the element of subjectivity and satisfying system of evaluation of practice teaching.

10

Continuing Professional Growth of Teachers — In-service Education

Teaching is one of the few professions in which a person starts working as a full-fledged professional soon after obtaining the professional qualification and sometimes even without this qualification. Engineers, doctors, business managers and even the I.A.S. personnel are not allowed to function as a full-fledged professional until they have undergone intensive education and training in their respective fields after completing the entry requirements of their job. As a consequence of scientific and technological advancements there has been not only explosion in knowledge but these have also brought about social consciousness and awareness of the need and importance of education. This has resulted in the horizontal and vertical expansion of education leading to expansion in the aims and objectives of education and thereby expansion in the curriculam and tasks and functions of the teachers. Today the teachers are not only expected to teach their subjects effectively to their students, they are also expected to contribute to the development of students' personality, to building up right attitudes, to stimulate and inspire students for free independent thinking, to function as responsible citizens, to enable them to face the problems of life.

It is now well known that the pre-service training/education of teachers is inadequate in the sense that it fails to equip the teachers with competencies to deal with the ever changing demands and tasks and functions of the teacher. This knowledge however is not new and the awareness has existed all through the years. Even before 1 started working as a teacher in a teacher-training college 38 years ago, there had been the talk of increasing the duration of the B.T./B.Ed course as it was felt that the course was too narrow, based on the unrealistic assumptions, and that the time of the course was too short to educate the prospective teacher in all that was needed to realize the continually expanding purpose of education. It has however not been possible to substantially change the course structure and requirements because of the constraints of time and many other considerations — financial and administrative, though there have been a few sporadic attempts at upgrading the curriculum and regulating the functioning of teacher training institutions. There is sadly no study to show how successful and effective these attempts have been to produce the type of teachers required to deal with the needs of the changing educational scene. The New Education Policy (1986) therefore has re-emphasized the need for reorganizing methods of recruitment to ensure merit, objectivity and continuity with spatial and functional targets, and has called for revitalization of teacher education through revision of curriculum and methods of teaching and evaluation procedures, and most of all through making training mode functional and motivational.

Teacher education like any other professional training is a continuous process and its pre-service and inservice components are inseparable. The inservice component for professionalization of teaching becomes all the more necessary and important when the pre-service course content has mostly remained unchanged, when the persons coming to the teaching profession are by and large rejectees from other coveted professions, are inadequate and found lacking in knowledge of their subject matter specialities. The in-service education of the teachers is the need of the time and it now occupies a key position in the efforts to bring about a significant improvement in school education. In-service education is expected not only to fill the gap/deficiency of pre-service teacher preparation but it also aims at continually updating and increasing the competencies of the teachers. The in-service education however has to be complimentary and not an alternative to the pre-service education programme.

In the backdrop of the limited functions and activities of pre-service teacher preparation, and also the experience of organization of programmes for preparation of workers in other professions, the value of an in-service education of teachers is now well recognized. When the in-service education programme is so important, it is necessary that the programme should be organized and administered on sound lines and in a manner that the objectives of in-service education for teachers are fully realized. It is generally agreed that the objectives of in-service education of teachers are basically to update the knowledge and skills of teachers and to bring about their professional growth, in other words, teacher development. Like all other branches of education, in-service education too, has three basic components *viz.* research, training and extension work, and each of these need to be attended to strengthen the in-service education programme for teachers.

Although the in-service education of teachers had been a topic of discussion and of some small vague action even during pre-independence years, definite programmes started being initiated only after the recommendations of the Secondary Education Commission (1952-53). Following the recommendations of Mudaliar Commissions, a network of Extension services centres attached to several teacher training colleges and university departments of Education were started in the attempt to bring about improvement in the quality and standards of school education. Alongside came up the State Institutes of Education (SIEs) which have now been upgraded into State Councils of Educational Research and Training (SCERT), one in each state to cover all levels of educational workers for in-service programmes.

At the national level a small beginning was made with the setting up of All-India Council for Secondary Education which was later expanded into Directorate of Education Programmes in Secondary Education (DEPSE). Another institution called the National Institute of Primary and Basic Education controlling the State Institutes opened in various states later also came up to cater to the needs of inservice education. It was however later felt that there should be a single strong national specialised body to cover all professional programmes in school education under one roof, and this was how the National Council of Educational Research and Training (NCERT) was started in 1961. Another organization now known as National Institute of Educational Planning and Administration began to look after the management orientation of school and college personnel.

The experience of the Extension Services Centres and later on when with the formation of NCERT the task of extension education was taken over by its Department of Field Services, had not been very productive. This had been so not because of lack of concern for reform and improvement of school education but because of the manner in which the in-service education need to be organized and conducted.

The National Policy on Education (NPE, 1986) while examining the educational activities in the country as a whole took note of the state of in-service education and came out with a plan for toning up the organization and functioning of in-service education. To this end, under the 1986 policy dispensation attempt was made to create an appropriate climate to generate initiative in school teachers for implementation of NPE, 1986 with the establishment of the institutions of DIETs (District Institutes of Education and Training), Institutes of Advanced Studies in Education (IASE), and Academic Staff Colleges. There was also initiated a programme of mass orientation of 5 lakh teachers — both primary and secondary, during vacations every year in about 10,000 camps with 50 teachers in each camp. For this, an in-service teacher education package consisting of separate modules of primary, upper primary and secondary teachers respectively was developed.

The DIETs have been conceived as one of the major steps towards effective teacher education. The DIETs are designed to improve and enrich the academic equipment of elementary school teachers, non-formal and adult education functionaries and other personnel at the lowest level of educational system. The DIETs aim at reaching out to the remotest parts of the country and making the teachers aware of the advantages of the educational knowhow in management and planning, in research and experimentation and in a variety of rich resources and learning materials.

The DIET is a step towards the decentralization of professional preparation and also the extension of excellence from urban to rural, from elite to the subaltern and from the higher to the lower level of education. It provides guidance and leadership in ensuring effective measures in the four aspects of universalization of elementary education (UEE) *viz.* (a) access, (b) enrolment (c) retention and (d) standards. It also facilitates the education and literacy of adults and of those who could not get into the formal system due to economic and social handicaps. While the existing teacher education institutions are largely concerned with only the pre-service teacher preparation, the DIET is based on the premise that teacher education is a continuous process and its pre-service and in-service components are inseparable. It assumes the role of organizing pre-service and in-service courses for not only the elementary school teachers but also for the personnel working in non-formal and adult education sector.

Major functions of the DIET are:

1. Pre-service and in-service education of elementary school teachers.
2. Continuing education of instructors and supervisors for non-formal and adult education, and providing general resource support to them.
3. Providing planning and management support for DBE (District Boards of Education), school complexes and educational institutions.
4. Serving as an evaluation centre for primary and upper primary schools as well as non-formal and adult education centres.
5. Making the provision of a resource and learning centre for teachers and instructors.
6. Providing educational technology and computer education support for the district.
7. Doing experimentation and research.

In order to perform its major functions effectively, the DIET consists of seven Academic Units. These are:

1. Pre-service teacher education.
2. In-service programmes and Extension services.
3. District Resource Unit for Adult and Non-formal Education.
4. Planning and Management.
5. Educational Technology.
6. Work-Experience.
7. Curriculum and Evaluation.

The institutes of Advanced Studies in Education (IASEs) are set up to offer both post-graduate and under graduate programmes at the pre-service level and to develop themselves into comprehensive institutions of teacher education offering programmes relevant to various stages of teacher education. Research, innovations and experimentation on teacher education are also to be taken up on a priority basis. The IASEs are expected to develop rich programmes of continuing teacher education at the elementary and secondary level, besides training personnel for preparation of software for educational technology. They will start diffrent types of courses in areas such as management, policy making, planning, extension and technology and also undertake advanced study of the theory of education, and conduct fundamental as well as applied research in education.

In addition to the above functions the IASEs will perform the following functions:

1. Conduct courses in elementary teacher education for graduates.
2. Prepare personnel for DIETs.
3. Prepare teacher educators at the elementary and secondary level.
4. Conduct in-service educations courses for elementary and secondary teacher educators.
5. Organize pilot programmes in Teacher Education.
6. Conduct advanced level fundamental and applied research and experimentation in education, specially of interdisciplnory nature.
7. Prepare research workers.
8. Organize training programmes for preparation of software and use of educational technology.

Keeping in mind the experiences of the Academic Staff Colleges, the IASEs and the DIETs in the organization and conduct of the in-service education programmes, in several of which the present writer had worked as a resource faculty, attempt is made to offer some suggestions that are likely to strengthen the functioning of the in-service education programmes and in the realization of the objectives of the programme. Underlying these suggestions is the assumption that both the organizers of the in-service education and its beneficiaries i.e. teachers are constantly in the process of learning and that they are learning from each other by interacting at professional level. Another fact that should be kept in mind is that providing in-service education to all teachers in elementary and secondary schools cannot be the responsibilities of a single agency. It requires the concerted and coordinated efforts of all the agencies and institutions engaged in the task of improving instruction in schools and providing for the professional growth of the teaching personnel. Such agencies include Colleges of Education, State Directorates of Education, SCERTs, NCERTs, DIETs, IASEs etc. Each of these agencies organizes various types of in-service programmes to meet the varying needs of teachers. There is hardly any coordination between them or any attempt to plan their programme jointly, in a systematic manner, taking into consideration the resources and the priorities so as to avoid duplication and waste. One way to achieve this coordination is to set up a central/nodal cell which should monitor the organizational aspect, programme content and the selection and activities of both the resource faculty and the participants in the in-service programme.

Having made these observations, it is suggested that all teachers need to undergo an in-service education programme to update their knowledge and skills and other competencies so as to survive in the academic world and to be adequate in discharging their tasks effectively and productively. It is not a secret that very few teachers try to go beyond the subject matter specialities, and here I quote the Statesman Survey Report (Jan. 10, 1985) "Far from doing extra reading, most do not bother to update their knowledge of their own subject and there are many senior faculty members who are ignorant of vast areas of their specialities. What people want is a 'world rolled into a capsule' and their need is served by 'quickies' on topical subjects." It is also a fact that even among those teacher educators who have earned their Ph.D. degrees, most have not pursued with their research as if the obtaining of the Ph.D degree was the be all and end all of their learning and educative process. The in-service education programme therefore should be made obligatory for all teachers irrespective of their standing in the professional ladder. However, the frequency and the duration of the programme for various categories of teachers can be worked out considering their administrative and educative feasibility.

Another suggestion follows from the first. It has been the experience of all of us teachers that when teachers are deputed to the in-service education programmes, and the expenses on training, boarding and lodging including the T.A. are borne by the sponsoring or organizing agencies the motivation to learn and profit from the in-service education programme, in most cases, becomes subservient to other temptations of paid holiday and social interactions. Hence, it would be worthwhile to consider that participants in the in-service programme besides being made compulsory for every teacher be also made a 'paid affair' in that if not the whole, atleast a part of the expenses on training is borne by the participants. The success of the in-service courses and programmes run by institutions like the Administrative Staff College of India, the IITs and the IIMs is a case in point behind making the above suggestion. Despite the fact that these institutions charge high fees, there is never a dearth of participants and the programmes are reported to benefit the participants professionally. Recently, this writer had the experience of addressing a group of participating teachers in a course on Effective Teaching Organized by the Institute of Capsule Psychological Courses and he found the group highly motivated, active and enthusiastic. Inspite of being a Sunday the attendance was full, these teachers had not been deputed by their institution, had come on their own and had paid quite a sum to participate and profit from the course. Needless to say that it will be possible only when the programme is meaningful and designed to meet the needs of the teachers, and there are incentives like promotional prospects and job satisfaction.

In the earlier section it has been stated that the in-service education component should compliment the pre-service education programme. In this connection it is felt that while the pre-service component should be broad based, the in-service education should be intensive and need based in that it should try to meet the needs of the teachers and the schools rather than be of a general nature both in content and approach. It should be better if a 'Capsule' type programme is developed and presented to teachers as there would not be much time available to teachers to participate in such programmes. It has been observed that in many a case the agencies dealing with these courses organize lectures that are more of a general nature, and often by resource faculty who may not be the right person for the job. To make the in-service education really worthwhile, the programme content should on the one hand be problem focussed and the faculty competent to deal with the problems and needs of the teachers. Lawrence et al. in conducting an analysis of 97 separate, well evaluated studies of in-service education, found that: programmes which have differentiated training experiences for diffrent teachers are more effective; programmes offering teachers opportunites to choose goals and activities are more effective; self directed training activities, while rare, tend to be successful; and programmes that linked the indvidual activities to a larger organization effort are also more effective. These findings and the fact that an in-service education programme brings in a variety of professional and teaching backgrounds and experiences, call for an individual approach to in-service education. Some approaches to differentiated in-service education which attempt to respond to the diverse needs of participants of in-service programmes can be as Harris suggests, intervisitations, field trips, internships, individual growth plans and teaching. Interactive video systems and computer assisted in-service are though being successfully used in the West, but it will take time to use these approaches meaningfully in our situation. However, in the West also a format which can meet the different needs of individuals in content depth, nature and pace in in-service education, as well as providing opportunities for group interaction and collaboration is scarce but attempts are being made to develop such modules.

Long term and continuous in-service education to the same group of teachers in their subject specialities is another step that will strengthen the functioning of in-service education. Organizers of in-service education should adopt a couple of institutions and provide in-service education to their teachers at frequent intervals so that there is also a follow-up and feed back from these teachers to the programme which may necessitate revision of the programme. These are only some of the measures that can strengthen the inservice education of teachers. The list is not exhaustive, but whatever measures are added, it will be possible to implement them only if there is sound infra-structure to run the in-service programme. An independent academic and administrative cell to organize such programmes, which will also continually engage in research concerning in-service education should go a long way in strengthening the in-service education of teachers. With institutions like DIETs, IASEs, SCERTs and NCERT, if they sincerely workout and manage the in-service education as defined for their organization and function, one can hope the goals of in-service education will not be difficult to realize.

The above observations however, are relevant when the in-service programmes are launched by the central and state agencies which cater mainly to government institutions. The private schools by and large, for one reason or the other, avoid participation in such programmes, though they do not deny the need and importance of continuous professional growth of their teachers.

School based in-service education of teachers (SBINSET) provide the best and the most economic plan/scheme for in-service education of teachers. In the school based local in-service becomes a part of a teacher's life and a segment of the usual work, and it does not take him away from his place of work, although occasional participation in the state and national level programmes acts as a refresher. In addition, the programme satisfies the nature of the in-service activity as a continuous affair. Learning from each others' experiences is the essence of this programme, though help from outside expertise is not a taboo, and can be taken advantage of whenever necessary and possible. The NCERT has recognized the relevance of the school based in-service programmes and included them in their on-going INSET programme. Many states, UTs and individual institutions all over the country have got gradually interested in the school based in-service education of teachers and one should expect the programme will gain sufficient popularity and strength in the years to come. The main area of discussion and consideration in this context centre around possible appropriate programmes and activities conducive to school basing of in-service programme. Some of these programmes can be thought of for (i) the entire staff, (ii) for the members of the various subject faculties and (iii) some for the self improvement of individual teachers.

The main plank of the school based programme is that every teacher is involved continuously in in-service education and professional growth.

In-service education of teachers has not been the concern of educational administrators, policy maker and planners in India alone. There has been a worldwide concern for this area of education and as a result a number of trends in in-service teacher training have been identified. The Information File published by the International Bureau of Education details the following trends in in-service education of teachers.

1 The effort to increase the effectiveness of in-service teacher training includes its integration into a system which combines two other important aspects of lifelong education, the pre-service education of teachers; and the daily experience of their working lives. It is expected that through pre-service training teachers will acquire suitable techniques for their continuing self-education.
2. Great attention be devoted to the creation and improvement of a system of incentives in order to make in-service training an integral component of the professional life of teachers.
3. Another significant trend is the effort to involve teachers more in decision-making process concerning the organization of in-service training courses. Participation in decision making is more strongly related to school focussed rather than teacher focussed in-service courses.
4. There is an evident tendency to focus the models of in-service teacher training more on the school. However, this does not mean the reduction of the teacher focussed models of in-service training. In the models of in service teacher training the development need of the school predominate. But this does not mean that these models should overlook the needs of particular groups or individuals within the school.
5 The tendency to try out innovatory methods of in-service training is of increasing importance. The choice reflects new problems which confront education systems and/or society, such as environmental education, health education, international education, computer and information

technology, and the solution of other so-called global problems.
6. Another trend is an increase in the duration of in-service teacher training, and mainly concerning the period set aside for the practical application of theoretical knowledge.
7. Generally, in-service teacher training serves, either explicitly or implicitly, as an instrument for change both in the education system and in society.

Daniel L. Duke analysed the researches on adult growth and development and his analysis revealed the following factors that can help explain why teachers are often indifferent to their own professional growth.

1. *Lack of awareness*: denying the need for growth, being out of touch with new developments in education, teachers do not set growth goals related to such development.

2. *Disillusionment*: seeing new initiatives dropped because of changes in leadership, priorities, or fundings; this results in loss of faith in the system's longterm commitment to change.

3. *Distrust*: questioning motives of those promoting changes; perception that administrators will not approve a goal unless it relates to their personal agenda.

4. *Pessimism*: pervasive feeling of helplessness, a belief that nothing an individual chooses to do will affect what happens to him or her.

5. *High comfort level with current practice*: believing that they have mastered the skills of teaching, reached a "comfort zone" where their lives are in balance.

6. *Pre occupation with other concerns*: being overwhelmed with other demanding concerns in personal or institutional life.

7. *Stress*: growth entails considerable stress resulting from increased choice: It is less stressful to be told what to do than to be faced with the choice of what kind of a person to be.

8. *Fear of failure*: growth involves a degree of risk, the possibility of not achieving a particular goal; teachers

either refrain from setting goals or set goals that can be easily achieved.

9. *Impatience*: growth is not a steady process of accomplishments, it is a matter of incremental progress and plateaus; teachers become impatient when they see a loss of momentum.

10. *Poor time management*: preception that professional growth is an extra, an add on, rather than an integral part of their work; hence the arangement that they are too busy with their regular duties to find time for growth-oriented activities.